PRIVATE PILOT'S
SURVIVAL MANUAL

Other TAB books by the author:

2209 *Computer Guide*
2251 *How to Take Great Photos From Airplanes*

PRIVATE PILOT'S
SURVIVAL MANUAL
BY FRANK KINGSTON SMITH

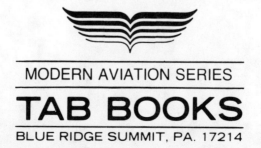

MODERN AVIATION SERIES

TAB BOOKS

BLUE RIDGE SUMMIT, PA. 17214

FIRST EDITION

FIRST PRINTING—OCTOBER 1979

Copyright © 1979 by TAB BOOKS

Printed in the United States of America

Library of Congress Cataloging in Publication Data

Smith, Frank Kingston.
    Private pilot's survival manual.

    Bibliography: p.
    Includes index.
    1. Survival (after airplane accidents, shipwrecks, etc.) I. Title.
TL553.7.S64   613.6′9   79-17327
ISBN 0-8306-9776-7
ISBN 0-8306-2261-6 pbk.

Preface

The purpose of this book is to help civilian lightplane pilots understand and assess the problems concerned with surviving until rescued if forced down in the wilderness of North America, from Mexico to Alaska, and the islands of the Caribbean and the Bahamas. The theme is that, if a problem is understood, anticipated and prepared for, survival and rescue are virtually assured. It will at least give you a new slant on the problems that pilots tend to dismiss from their minds.

Hopefully, none of us will ever have to go through a wilderness survival experience, but if we do, it will certainly pay off to have prepared for the emergency. There is an old Western adage to the effect that a man may carry a gun for years and years without needing it, but when the time comes that he *does* need it, he needs it damn badly and the biggest gun is none too big. As you read this discussion, keep that philosophy in mind, except that for the word "gun," you should substitute the words "survival kit."

Frank Kingston Smith

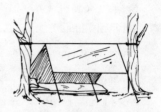

Contents

Introduction 9

1 Mental Preparations 15
Fear—Thinking Ahead—What Is "The Wilderness"—Survivable
Aircraft Accidents—Emergency Landings—Types of Emergency
Landings—Psychological Preparation—The Survivable Land-
ing—Slow and Gentle—Rapid, Progressive Deceleration is the
Key—Flaps and Gear—Landing On the Treetops—Pick Your Best
Spot—Conclusions

2 An Overview of Survival Problems 33
Requirements for Survival—The Fear of the Unknown—About
First Aid—Typical Injuries—Shock and Its Treatment—Typical
Illnesses—Setting Up Housekeeping, Basic Instructions—First
Things First—The Basic Survival Kit—Commercial Basic Survival
Kits—Our Grab Bag Survival Kit—Commercial Survival Kits for
Heavy Going—However...—Compromises Compromises

3 Meeting the First Requirement: Water 51
The Need for Water—Water Conservation—Water Availability—Water in the Desert—Desert Water Sources—Portable
and Potable

4 Meeting the Second Requirement: Shelter 57
Staying in the Airplane—Keeping Comfortable—Foul Weather
Gear—Lean-to Construction—Natural Shelters—About Tents—
Tube Tents—Survival Clothing—Hot Weather Clothing—Cold
Weather Clothing—From the Skin Out—Comfort at Night—
Sleeping Bags—A Last Word About Sleeping Bags—... And About
Mattresses—...And About Bed Clothing

5 Meeting the Third Requirement: Fire **74**
The Basic Need For Fire—Laying a Fire in the Woods—Fire-
Laying Tools—A Few Words About Edged Tools—Camp Fires—
Fire Starting—Kitchen Match Preparation—Fire Starting Back-
Ups—Keep Your Tinder Dry—Flint and Steel, Etc.—But When It
Rains and Blows...—And Then, There's...—Back to Cooking
Fires—Other Types of Stoves—Signalling Fires—Colored Smoke

6 Meeting the Fourth Requirement: Food **89**
Food Required—Food Availability—Berries, Roots, Seeds
Local Food Availability—Other Treats From the Sea—Other
Natural Foods—Fresh Fish—Fresh Meat—Game Getting

7 Survival Guns **99**
A Few Basics—Shoulder Guns For Survival—Ubiquitous and
Ample—Combination Guns—Handguns For Survival—Pistol
Pros and Cons—The Cons...—The Morale FActor—Advice About
Hunting—It's Not That Easy—Some Basic Hints—Bird
Hunting—Practice—Preparing Fish and Small Game—Cleaning
Procedures—Large Animals—Butchering—Cooking in the
Wilds—With No Pot to Put Water In—Aluminum Foil—Survival
Knives—...And Sharpening Them—An Alternative Approach—
Reconstitutable Goods

8 Our Survival Kit **127**
Aircraft Survival Kits-Generally—The Fair Weather Survival
Kit—Our Big Red Bag

9 How About Walking Out? **134**
The Natural Urge to "Do Something"—Avoiding the Problem in the
First Place—A Daniel Boone, You Ain't—The Mechanics of
Walking—Walking the Rough—Climbing Hills—Other Hazards on
the Trail—However...—Navigating on Foot—The Magnetic
Compass—Always Leave Notes

10 Down At Sea **147**
Simulation—Floatation Gear—Wear the Equipment!—Briefing
Time—Check Your Equipment!—Realistic Practice—Ditching
Procedures—Call For Help Right Away—After the Splash—
Exposure Problems at Sea—And Then, There's Seasickness—All
You Can Do Is Wait—Special Signalling Devices—Water Markers

11 Initiating Rescue Operations **166**
The First Step—Set Up An "Overdue Alert—Flight Plans—
Personal Telephone Calls—The Pay-off

12 How Are They Going to Find You? **169**
The First Line—The Second Line—Possible Radio Com-
munications—Close-in Visual Signals—Pyrotechnics, etc.

13 Happy Ending **178**

Appendix A **183**

Appendix B **185**

Index **189**

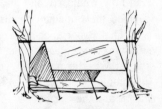

Introduction

It is human nature to believe that one's future will be largely pleasant, placid and untroubled, or, to put it another way, that accidents will only happen to someone else. However, with the addition of layers of age and experience, one becomes more of a realist and takes steps to avoid various forms of personal injury by learning what the "hazard problems"—a phrase borrowed from the law—are, then creating a defense against them. Accident-free automobile operators learn the technique of "defensive driving," which someone once described as developing the mental attitude that everyone else is insane and trying to kill you. All aircraft pilots take certain pre-flight precautions as a matter of training: they drain fuel sumps, check oil levels and the general appearance of the aircraft they are about to fly, including a visual inspection of the engine. But a very small percentage of lightplane pilots prepare ahead of time to cope with the aftermath of a forced landing far from civilization and immediate aid. Most of us don't even think about it when we hit the starter switch to begin a 500 or 1,000 mile trip, whether for business or pleasure. Confident that our light twins and single-engine airplanes will carry us at three miles a minute over mountains, lakes, forests and deserts, we just load our suitcases in the luggage compartment, as we would load the trunk of the family car, and go.

A couple of years ago, a personal experience jolted my psyche. Three of us had arranged to fly to the Province of Ontario in my Cherokee Six, then have a Canadian bush pilot fly us by his floatplane into a lonely lake in the region north of Georgian Bay where, it was

9

rumored, one could walk across the water on the backs of a multitude of lake trout. In my mind's eye, I will see forever that little floatplane rising from the lake where it had left us for a week on our own, then turning in a southerly direction. As the sight and sound of that Cessna Skytruck dwindled and disappeared I felt an overwhelming sense of loneliness. What, I wondered, would happen to our trio if that pilot, for some reason, did not come back in seven days and pick us up? Would we, or could we survive until we were rescued? And how would anyone find us on one lake of the thousands that dappled the Canadian countryside?

That experience was really the genesis of my concern about surviving a forced landing in the wilderness. Although my wife and I spent the better part of 20 years hop-scotching the North American continent, from Canada to Mexico and the islands of the Atlantic, Pacific and the Caribbean, the only times we carried survival equipment as such was on our over-water trips, which meant "floatation gear:" inflatable life preservers (Mae Wests) and an inflatable life raft. We had flown from Coast to Coast and border to border dozens of times, carrying no more than our suitcases and camera equipment. Then after more than 7500 hours of trouble-free flying in the log—which translates into more than a million miles—I had in quick succession a couple of experiences that put the problem into better perspective and got me thinking of preparing to deal with the distasteful possibility of a forced landing far from immediate help.

The first thought-provoking episode came on a late fall flight from Dallas to Denver. My co-pilot wife, Marianne, and I had been advised by Dallas Flight Service that all en route and terminal forecasts were favorable for making the trip under visual flight rules. According to our charts and computer the 495-nautical/575-statute mile flight would take about three hours and 45 minutes and we had a total of five plus forty of useable fuel in the tanks (82 gallons). What was more, since we, out of an abundance of caution plan on the basis of "net fuel", i.e.: 75% of what is available (in our case, 61 gallons) which means landing and topping off at four plus 20, we had more than enough go-juice to make the trip non-stop. When we got to Denver, we would have 29½ gallons on board: more than two hours of reserve, so if Denver was for some reason closed, we could fly somewhere else within 300 miles. As we figured it, we had an "out"; a soft feather bed to land on. It was, we thought, a piece of cake. So off we went, without even filing a visual flight plan.

Following airways to keep well clear of the military flight training areas to the west, we went over Oklahoma City an hour and seven minutes after taking off from Love Field—right on the money on our estimate. The 116-nm leg to Gage, however, took 58 minutes, instead of the 51 we had computed, indicating that our ground speed had dropped to 118-kts/138-mph instead of the 135/158 we had estimated, which hinted that we had encountered an unexpected headwind. But, since the sky was absolutely clear and the air was as smooth as silk, I assumed (as husbands will) that my wife had simply miscalculated (and told her so), then pointed the spinner at Lamar, Colorado 175-nautical/202-statute miles up the line, on a direct, off-airways course.

Marianne, nettled by my critical observations relating to her competence as a navigator, had diligently recomputed our estimated time for the leg as one plus 20 (leaving a minute or two for fumble room), but the leg actually took an hour and 45 minutes, which worked out to a groundspeed of 98-knots/104-mph—a *hell*ova headwind! According to the Jepp charts, we had 135-nautical/158-statute miles still to go and had already flown for three hours and 50 minutes, only a half an hour short of our self-imposed "net fuel" limit. If I had had as many as three brain cells working, I would have turned around and landed at Lamar to refuel, but I didn't. On the basis that we still had two and a half hours of fuel in the tanks, I pressed on. Hell, if our groundspeed dropped to 80-knots/93-mph we would still be at Denver in another hour.

Boy, the mistakes in judgment I made *that* day!

Inching along only a couple of thousand feet above the terrain—remember, it is almost a mile above sea level in the area—I eyeballed and can report that the earth below was as bleak, inhospitable and forbidding as the face of Mars. I was looking it over because between Lamar and Denver we were too low for radio communications and all four fuel gauges were nudging the empty marks, which always makes me nervous. For some reason, I tuned in to Denver Approach Control, just in time to hear the pilot of a high-flying jet airliner ask the air traffic controller to confirm that Denver was having a blizzard and that all airfields in the area were closed. Puckertime had arrived.

Up by Kiowa, I turned left and headed for Colorado Springs in a crosswind that had the Cherokee Six ambling along on the bias, like a cocker spaniel, while I waited every moment for the engine to quit on a dry tank, so I could switch to another one—and hope that the engine would catch, which can be a problem with fuel injected engines.

We made it, all right, and the tanks took only 63 gallons, which meant that we still had an hour and 20 minutes' worth left. But, as I washed the cotton out of my mouth with a libation at the Broadmoor bar, I wondered what the outcome might have been if we had not heard that airline pilot's query. What would I have done if we had run out of fuel over that harsh, craggy area? And how we could have perished before anyone found us.

A few months later, I had another experience, this time on a hop from San Antonio to El Paso, Texas. Again, it was well within our conservative restriction: 434-nm/505-sm, or three hours and 15 minutes.

This time, we knew that we were going to have a strong northerly wind, but no matter. The first leg from San Antonio to Junction was strictly routine and took about 40 minutes. But a few minutes out of Junction, we lost the VOR navigation signal and had to dead reckon our way until we picked up the Ft. Stockton VOR signal. Except that, we never did receive Ft. Stockton, *or* Pecos, *or* Midland. We were, as far as I was concerned, lost. And once again, the vast expanse of rocky, uninhabited, arid land below—and stretching out to the horizon—made me wonder, What if?

By tacking into the wind another ten degrees, and grimly holding a compass heading for two hours, during which mile high mountains slid by under our wings, we finally intercepted a wide highway, which was comforting, and in a few more minutes El Paso's electronic signal was strong enough to lead us directly in—from the southeast. I really believe that for at least part of that trip, we were over Mexico.

When we returned to our home base in Washington, D.C., I dug out all of my camping-technique books, including my old Boy Scout Manual, and obtained the official Air Force and Navy Survival Manuals, which I perused carefully, Then I began to assemble all of the literature available on the subject of post-crash survival and took an extension course at the local high school on How to Rough It in the Woods.

From the beginning of my serious study of the existing publications I was disappointed by the heavy military aviation orientation even in the books supposedly addressed to civilian pilots: constant references to parachutes and how the parachute materials can be used to create tents and sleeping bags and the shroudlines used for everything from clothes lines to mountain climbing ropes. Besides I soon found myself yawning and turning several pages at a time because I really don't care about the specific issues of survival in the Gobi or Sahara deserts, to the jungles of Africa or the Matto Grosso, or how to cope with the natives of New Guinea or setting up escape programs from enemy-held territory. It did not seem to me that such information would mean anything to the owners and pilots of the hundreds of thousands of light, personally-flown airplanes in the United States, Canada, Mexico or the Bahamas/Caribbean region.

I must also confess to what appears a heresy, as far as survival book writers are concerned: I simply cannot see any value in the (frequently beautifully drawn) pen and ink representations of edible—or inedible—plants, bushes, trees, nuts, berries, roots, or what have you. It seems absurd to present this kind of information to laymen, particularly to pilots downed in the wilderness and not fully prepared to wander around in the vicinity of their wrecked airplanes, book in hand, studying local flora to determine what can or can not be eaten. Those black and white drawings, artistic though they may be, will not transform anyone of my acquaintences into an instant botanist. As far as that goes, neither would a complete book of four-color illustrations.

It did not take long to recognize the pattern of most survival type books: How to Start Fires (flint and steel; focussing the sun's rays by a magnifying glass or a watch crystal filled with water); How to Build a Shelter (pin boughs; blocks of snow); ditto Beds (pine boughs, again, plus digging a little trench in the still-warm bed of a recent campfire) and Food Gathering (edible berries, plants, grubs and various wildlife, including birds, bunnies and porcupines, along with ways to create snares and traps to catch them). I became conversant with the techniques of making birch bark canoes and dugouts hewed from trees. Government manuals seemed too detailed on such subjects and also dwelt at length on surviving on polar ice packs and ovenlike deserts, usually in enemy-held territory, anticipating a lengthy stay.

None of this information did much for me. First, I cannot picture myself, prowling the woods stalking the wild asparagus or any other edible plants, particularly if something else is available. Besides, military manuals assumed that the aviators and sailors would already be at least to some degree equipped to handle survival situations, since they routinely carry with them survival packets and emergency equipment including radio locator transmitters, fire-making tools, foul weather gear, warm clothing and *food*. If they run out of food, they usually have the means with them in their survival kits to obtain more food, either fish or game, whereas, like most private pilots, my wife and I tended to take off on a long cross country trip armed only with our own suitcases, plus maybe a sandwich or two, a can of soft drinks and an apple. When I read about cutting down some ridgepole pines to make a shelter or bed of boughs on which one might loll, gorging on wild berries before a roaring fire, the thought crossed my mind: With *what*?

The answer came together when I was reading a how-to book for automobile camping, and what one should take (drive) into the woods for a week of being in the outdoors, of roughing-it in style. It seemed to me that there should be some way to survive in style and comfort until we are found and rescued.

This book tells about what we did, and why, to make it possible.

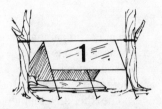

Mental Preparations

Sitting up there in the soft blue sky, whizzing across the face of the land at the rate of two or three miles a minute in our lightplanes as we have done so many times in the past, few of us give much thought to the possibility of having to descend and land before reaching our intended destination. Once a pilot has logged a few thousand trouble-free miles of cross country flying to remote and glamorous vacation and recreation spots, or flies regularly for business, a tremendous confidence develops that the machine will complete the present flight as successfully as it completed the last one.

This is not an unreasonable attitude, for that is precisely what does happen in real life, most of the time. Let's face it, no one would embark on any kind of a lengthy journey, whether it be by the family car, a boat, a personal airplane—or the larger "mass transportation" versions: bus, train, ship, airliner—if he really believed that the odds were in any way against an uneventful, successful completion of the trip. Every year millions of people pack into automobiles and go off on tours of the North American Continent without giving a thought to the fact that statistics show that a couple of football stadiums could be filled with the bodies of automobile occupants that have been killed or injured on the nation's highways. Any driver on the Interstate Highway System will attest to the fact that cars loaded down to the frame roar along at high speeds, their drivers obviously not giving a thought to the possibility of a tire blowout, or a collision with another vehicle. On two lane highways, cars pass in opposite directions frequently with closure speeds of 100 miles an hour or more,

15

separated from oncoming traffic only by a four inch wide line painted on the roadway. Yet, all of these hazards are mentally rejected by automobile drivers, or to put it another way, the clear potential for accidents is accepted as natural, normal and commonplace—as a fact of life. The mental attitude of most civilian pilots is directly comparable. We have no fear, no anxiety about making a trip in our airplanes. This leads to a peculiar psychological situation. When suddenly gripped by fear, we are not prepared to cope with it or its side-effects.

Fear

Fear is a fundamental emotion which produces many physiological changes on one's body whenever one perceives a threat to his well-being, especially to his life. Once the nature of the phenomenon is understood and anticipated, a course of action can be planned to overcome the development of an *unreasoning* fear, or panic, whenever one is faced with an emergency situation. By training to cope with an emergency, anyone's chances for surviving it are tremendously improved. That is precisely why airline pilots take emergency procedures training every six months; if an emergency develops they are mentally prepared to accept the *reality* of the emergency and to react to it by taking an appropriate course of action. Note the word, "reality." One of the most difficult mental attitudes to overcome is the psychological refusal to acknowledge that the situation is deteriorating, until it is too late to make an intelligent or thought-out decision.

What we are talking about here is the prevention of panic, or mindless random behavior in reacting to an emergency condition, whether it is instantaneous—such as a sudden loss of engine power—or protracted, as would be the situation of having to spend some time in the wilderness, far from what we consider civilization. An awareness that such a stay may be for several days or even for several weeks would tend to influence the exercise of a pilot's judgment, particularly if he knows that he is unequipped to contend with it.

On the other hand, as long as one does not feel helpless and without hope, he can make intelligent, thought-out decisions and it is axiomatic that being able to respond with a cool head and in a disciplined fashion to abnormal situations makes survival more of a certainty, no matter what kind of emergency is encountered.

Thinking Ahead

In forced landing situations in the wilderness, there is a real and present requirement for survival equipment and for the ability to be

Not all ditching is done at sea. Here is an airplane that ditched in a small, shallow lake in New England. Rule One in ditching is to be sure that the door is open before the airplane strikes, and that it is somehow propped open, so water pressure will not close it and keep it closed. Courtesy NTA, Accidental Investigation School

able to use it, all of which we will get to in a moment. But the most important aspect in any survival situation is the intensity of one's *will to survive* and the determination not to be overcome by the situation into which he has been thrust. With this mental attitude plus the equipment and know-how of bringing it off, intelligent, reasoned decisions can be made that will lead to rescue. Remember the motto of the Boy Scouts: BE PREPARED.

Although most of us take off from and land at properly designated and licensed airports or airstrips, reasonably level, free of ruts and holes, frequently hard-surfaced, and never would consider landing anywhere else, we must not overlook the fact that, not so long ago, everyone flew from grass fields if for no other reason than that there were few designated airports. When contemplating the necessity for making an off-airport landing, keep in mind that it can frequently be done without injuring the airplane at all, and that frequently the airplane may be severely damaged without any serious injuries to the occupants, which makes the survival situation somewhat easier to bear.

What is "The Wilderness"?

Wilderness has a variety of meanings, depending on who you ask, ranging from "nature in the raw" to Death Valley, but essentially it is a generic term describing an uncultivated region, uninhabited by man. It does not have to be barren, empty wasteland, as many people believe. Mankind has adapted to surviving and propogating itself in many locales and conditions that many people would consider totally uninhabitable wilderness: Eskimos who live within the Arctic Circle where it would seem that nothing could survive the cold and lack of greenery; inhabitants of the immense waterless deserts of the world; the Incas and their descendents who lived in the bitter cold, high altitudes of Chile. Many regions that seem barren to city-folk are however—if not teeming—supplied by complicated food chains which support a wide variety of animal life.

When you get right down to it, there are only a few types of terrain and climate that we may be required to cope with in survival situations: mountains, praries, rolling country and deserts, with varying amounts of precipitation, depending on the season of the year. As for the latter, survival is a great deal easier in mild or warmish weather, but becomes somewhat more complex in extremely hot climate (especially if water is in short supply) and is a real problem when the temperatures at night drop to the discomfort range. For survival purposes some regions can be described as "friendly" to a downed airman who must live there until rescued, and others, depending on all factors involved, can be described only as hostile. Our purpose is to prepare to come to grips with the most hostile circumstances we may encounter on any particular flight. The most important aspect of this is to be able to survive the landing.

Survivable Aircraft Accidents

The National Transportation Safety Board, which is charged with investigating and determining the probable cause for fatal aircraft accidents, initially categorizes all accidents into two groups: survivable and non-survivable. Examining the NTSB files, including photographs of airplane crashes and interviewing accident investigators has led me to the same conclusion held by most of them: those involving a direct *head-on* collision with an unyielding object (a mountain, a building, a stone fence or the ground, as in a straight-in crash) at flying speed—over 80 mph—are usually fatal. But most accidents involving a glancing, shearing, sideswipe which knocks pieces and parts off the airplane so that it decelerates quickly with the cabin area intact result in the airplanes' occupants emerging with little more than a severe shaking up. Remember that! As we shall get to later, the most important thing for a pilot facing an emergency landing is to *keep the airplane flying under control* until it touches down. That is absolutely imperative.

Sometimes an aircraft landed lightly on the tops of trees in a forest will stay there. In this case the occupants had to be rescued with a ladder and cherry-picker. Courtesy Vermont State Police.

While I am at it, let me caution that going over the summary reports of aircraft accidents, as issued by NTSB, can be very misleading to anyone lacking the experience and background to interpret them in the light of real life operations. For example, many of the accident reports which contribute to general aviation's total show that the pilots involved were involved in frequently bizzare ways of breaking all of the operational rules imposed by the Federal Aviation Administration and the exercise of so-called common sense, ranging from hand-propping an airplane to start it—with no competent pilot at the controls—to proceeding from the local pub to an airplane and busting it forthwith. Strange, the reports of pilot-drinking accidents are used by the press to conclude that a great many private pilots are drinking and flying, which is not so. The *proper* interpretation is that if a guy takes a few then goes flying, the odds are that he is going to have an accident directly as a result of alcohol impairment of his senses and reaction time. In other words, the statistics show that drinking and flying will kill a pilot, not that the pilots en mass are all sloshed up all the time.

Few accidents are attributed to mechanical failures. Most come about as a result of unwarranted low flying ("buzzing" to show off; airbatics; flying cross country or down a river at 100 feet and hitting high tension wires), from "fuel mismanagement", which simply means running the tanks dry en route—certainly the *dumbest* thing any airman can do—or "continuing into adverse weather conditions," which means an unqualified pilot, not instrument-rated as required by law, has flown into cloud and lost control of the airplane, usually with fatal results. Far too many accident reports concern pilots who have tried to make the airplane do something it cannot do and keep flying, such as a steep turn at slow airspeed, or attempting to make a go-around to salvage a botched approach, or making a too-steep climb immediately after take-off. In all three of these situations, the wing will become stalled and a stall/spin fatal accident is in the making. When you consider that a stall and resulting spin from an altitude, say, of 200 feet is roughly equivalent to driving a car off the top of a 20 story building, the lethal aspects, or as they say at NTSB the "non-survivalibility" of such accidents becomes clear.

Emergency Landings

Approximately one-quarter of the total of lightplane accidents reported are associated with emergency landings or unplanned landings off designated airports and few of them, although they must be reported because of the extent of damage to the airplane, are fatal, and in most cases the occupants walk away unscathed. Moreover, a number of forced landings made each year never do reach the memory banks of NTSB's computer, simply because no one is hurt and no damage is done to the aircraft involved. As a case in point, in the early years of my flying career I made several emergency landings, in that I landed short of my intended destination on a more or less *ad hoc* basis for a variety of reasons.

Before I was instrument-rated my instructor told me forcefully that I was never, never, *never* to enter a low visibility condition or fly at night and that I should make the decision as early as possible either to go back or, if that was not possible, to land somewhere while I could see what I was doing. Several times when I found myself confronted with deteriorating weather such as heavy clouds, thunderstorms, ground fog or premature darkness, I landed literally on cow pastures, once spending the night in the airplane (a Cessna 140). I landed on a hard packed ocean beach when a line of thunderstorms swept through the area and I couldn't find anywhere else to run and hide. Another time I landed on the then-new Garden State Parkway near a telephone booth, so I could call the weatherman and find what was developing that wasn't in the original forecast. On each occasion the "forced" landing and ensuing departure were uneventful although I spent most of one night on a remote Florida ranch chasing steers away from my fabric-covered Tri-Pacer which the bovine critters seemed to regard as some sort of manna from heaven, a hors d'ouvre de cow.

This aerial view, taken on an actual search and rescue mission, indicates the problems of locating an aircraft that has gone down in the woods without signalling equipment. The wreck is at the left-center of the photo.

Subsequent to each incident, I fired up the engine, took off and went on my way, a little behind schedule, but safe and sound. Naturally no such incidents show up in NTSB statistics, since both the pilot and the airplane remained unbent. It is difficult to make a statistical record of things that don't happen.

Of course, there is always the chance of receiving a violation from the FAA for making an off-airport landing, but this is nothing to be of concern in a valid emergency situation, because everyone concerned would rather have you whole than becoming a victim by virtue of trying to stretch your flight to a real airport. It must be a recognized emergency, though, for some suspicious FAA types frown at any barnstorming activities.

One day my old friend and fellow airplane degenerate, Paul Parker (a radio broadcaster in New York when not aviating for the fun of it) was chugging up the coastline of New Jersey in his impeccably kept Fairchild 24 which was built about 1936 and powered by an equally venerable straight-six, inverted Ranger engine. Well aware that the airframe and engine were aged longer than most whiskies, Paul was brought to full alert when the Ranger began to hiccup in the vicinity of Sandy Hook and elected to essay an immediate landing on the nearest smooth area. Obviously the beach stretching out was his selection and soon he flared out to a three-point landing, rolling-out nicely until a wheel sank into a soft spot with which the pretty monoplane gracefully went up on its nose and stayed there, looking like the gnomon of a huge sundial. It took some doing to remove the airplane back to its native heath and repaired, at a cost of several of Paul's pesos. And—you guessed it—Paul received one of those chummy letters from the FAA about making an off-airport landing. He had a time convincing them that it was for real.

What I am getting at is that not all forced landings result in damage to an airplane or its occupants. Since I assume that we agree on the point that the primary objective is to come through the landing without personal injury, that is another point to bear in mind.

Types of Emergency Landings

Strictly speaking, an emergency may be defined alternatively as (1) a sudden, generally unexpected occurrence, or (2) a set of circumstances demanding immediate action. Aviation applications involving returning to *terra firma* under either of these definitions are commonly known as "emergency landings," but may be divided into two specific and somewhat different sub-groupings: *forced* landings and *precautionary* landings.

A forced landing may be defined as an immediate landing made necessary because the airplane, although aerodynamically controllable, is unable to continue flight, as in the case of the loss of engine power (thrust), for whatever reason, from catastrophic break-up to running out of fuel. Of the thousands of emergency ("forced") landing I have examined over the last 20 years, a very low percentage has been due to actual engine structure failures and in most of those cases the engine was still capable of producing partial power—enough to fly on until a controlled landing could be made. My oldest son had a hole burn through a piston in a light single one night, and by remaining cool and professional was able to fly it back to the airport he had just departed from, with the engine bucking and shaking. A pilot must be proficient in handling abnormal in-flight situations and not panicked by them. Not all pilots meet these requirements.

Last summer I heard a pilot aloft screaming for help because he had lost an engine in a light twin (an Aztec). From 8,500 feet, he was unable to control the airplane, and did not shut down the left engine until he was down to 2,000 feet, all the while going around and around in a huge descending spiral. Then in a remarkable exhibition of aeronautical ineptness, barely able to keep the airplane under control (all of which made me wonder how he had received his multi-engine rating in the first place) he stumbled towards and made a straight-in approach to the nearest airport with mile-long runways, and proceeded to land, gear-up. Although he had shoved the gear

Another light twin down in the woods with minor injuries to two occupants. The wings and empennage sheared off, but the cabin area remained intact. (Courtesy Pennsylvania Bureau of Aviation)

handle to the extend-gear position on final approach, he had over-looked (if ever he had known) the fact that, when he shut down the left engine, he had cut off the hydraulic pump. The airplane skidded down the concrete for 1500 feet, showering the area with sparks all the way, and was extensively damaged. And you know what? There was nothing wrong with the left engine! What had happened was that the fuel primer for the left engine had come unlocked, which always screws up the fuel pressure and makes the engine run rough because of uneven fuel distribution. Emergency landing? Forced landing? That's how it went into the books, although it was a sound airplane, flown by an incompetent pilot who went into panic immediately. Any pilot worth his salt knows the engine-roughness drill: check magnetos, switch fuel tanks, check primer locks, change mixture settings and power settings, and *keep the airplane flying under control*. A pilot's poise—sometimes described as "grace under pressure"—can sometimes eliminate the need for an immediate forced landing, which is the worst type, since the pilot just about has to take the landing area as he finds it and has to do everything right the first time. Someone asked one of the astronaut-pilots of the Space Shuttle what he would do if the approach was messed up on the return to earth.

"Well," he replied thoughtfully. "One thing about it, y'ain't going to go around."

The second class of emergency landings, the precautionary landing, is far more common and entirely different from the sudden, irretrievable power-loss cases. In precautionary landing situations the definition quoted ("a set of circumstances demanding immediate action") should be amended to read "...demanding immediate *decision*," and may be characterized by factors or symptoms indicating the need to make a premeditated landing, whether on or off an airport, because continuing the flight may be possible but is inadvisable because it clearly cannot be completed as planned. Making a decision to land because of encountering bad weather or running low on fuel results in precautionary landings which are made with engine power available, although the landing is not made on an airport, but somewhere in the wilderness. This book will deal with all types of emergency landings, but it is recommended that, when it is clear to a pilot that he is going to have to descend, it is better to make the descent, approach and landing, no matter where, with power.

Psychological Preparation

There is a quirk of human nature that must be trained-out of all of us: the refusal to accept that an imminent hazard exists, or that the situation may rapidly get out of hand. In the case of pilots, this mental block gets worse (or harder to overcome) with increasing time logged of successful, non-incident affected flights. This is why airline pilots go through a complete biannual emergency procedure drill, alternating sessions in a real airplane and, six months later, a highly sophisticated flight simulator which can duplicate every situation that an airplane can produce. Being mentally prepared to deal with a situation makes a whale of a lot of difference when one actually develops. That is why the layers of confidence built up in the thinking of high-time pilots lead to them rejecting the idea that there may be a problem afoot until it is too late to do anything about it. Many cases on record show pilots pressing on when they might have made successful precautionary landings; instead, they kept going until they ran out of fuel and had to make power-off landings, which converts a precautionary landing situation into a real forced landing. It takes enormous poise to make the decision early.

Another aerial shot, taken from a S & R aircraft. The Cessna was landed at its slowest practicable airspeed (note full flap position) and simply turned over. Three occupants were taken out by helicopter; only one had any injuries, and those minor. Courtesy FAA

The Survivable Landing

Developing a *tough mental attitude* will enable you to make the decision to make that precautionary off-airport landing and to execute it with as few injuries as possible—even though it means sacrificing the airplane. More people have been killed or seriously injured trying to "save the airplane" than by almost any contributing factor in the annals of accident recording. You must remember the instructions that were so firmly planted in your head when you were first landing to fly: "If the engine quits on take-off, land it straight ahead." Why? Because if you are flying at a slow airspeed and try to get back to the airport from which you have just departed by making a steep turn, that very maneuver increases the stalling speed of the wing and you will almost surely spin in, straight down, just as so many people have done in the past, invariably with fatal results. But, if upon losing power you push the nose over, keep up flying speed in a power-off glide and land—no matter where—at the minimum ground speed, the odds of your surviving are immeasurably increased.

Exactly the same reasoning applies to an engine-out approach and landing in the wilderness. If we eliminate those really violent head-on smashes into mountains or the ground because of loss of control in instrument flight meteorological conditions, which NTSB describes as being caused by "continued VFR flight into adverse weather conditions," most off-airport forced landings do not come as a surprise to the pilot. Putting it another way, a tough-minded pilot will know that the flight is not going to be completed as originally planned and, if he has his wits about him, will have time to fly around looking for suitable terrain on which to land, in many cases even to "drag" likely looking sites before essaying a landing. From 5,000 feet, although there is no engine power, a lightplane pilot has some 300 square miles within his gliding range—and vision. With partial power, he has more than that, because he can extend his glide angle.

Since most lightplanes can touch down at 50 to 60 mph—which is to say "at normal highway speeds"—they can be landed on a reasonably smooth surface and will decelerate quickly but smoothly be shedding parts along the way, which will absorb energy. Unless the airplane hits something solid head-on, it will usually come to rest with no more than minor injuries to the occupants. There is a big "IF" here, perhaps I should say two big "IFs." The first is IF the occupants are all firmly strapped in, *including* shoulder harness and lap belts. The second is, IF there is nothing loose in the cabin, including luggage, seats, portable radios, cameras and chart cases. Everything not strapped down becomes a missile which can do great physical damage. We recommend cargo nets and luggage straps or other security devices. In any event, there are numerous reports of off-airport forced landings where the occupants have escaped unscathed, including landings in forests, deserts, on mountainsides and on sandbars in rivers, only to die of "exposure" because they were not equipped to protect themselves against the forces of Nature. It is also interesting that few off-airport landings in the wilds result in fires.

Slow and Gentle

The most important aspect of making any landing of an emergency nature is to approach, flare and land at the slowest controllable airspeed, but above all, it *must* be a controlled landing with the wing flying until the very end, not allowing a stall/spin situation to develop, with its usually messy aftermath. Once on final approach for the landing on the spot selected, the course of flight should be straight ahead, with no sudden or erratic course changes, especially no steep turns. If you practice flying your airplane in all speed regimes, approaching the stall carefully under the tutelage of a good flight instructor, you will be able to nail down the stalling airspeed, which in most lightplanes is somewhere around 50 to 55 mph. Hence, if you make an emergency into a 15 mph wind, you will be traveling across the ground at about the same speed cars drive on city streets. If you remember that momentum increases with the square of the velocity, you will realize that if you land at 55 mph you will require only one-fourth of the decelerative force to stop than if landing at 105 mph.

Rapid, Progressive Deceleration is the Key

The very quick—but not instant—deceleration that is a prerequisite for surviving a wilderness landing is created by the nature of the aircraft structure itself, for as parts are stripped off or crushed by impact with objects on the ground, the aircraft is slowing. The conclusion after studying large numbers of aircraft accidents is that, unless the fuselage hits something immovable head-on, that the collapsing of the soft metal, almost "tear-away" structure—wings, empennage, landing gear—especially when combined with the frictional arresting power of shrubs, small trees, or furrows in the ground will stop the airplane quickly, yet the occupants will step out unhurt. Anyone who has participated in naval aircraft carrier operations knows that planes moving across a deck at 120 mph can be snubbed to a stop within a few feet time and time again, with no ill effects on the airmen, who are of course well strapped in. So, if you do find that you have to land off an airport, be sure that your passengers are all well strapped in and that they have some kind of padding—overcoats, cushions, soft luggage, towels—in front of their faces, eyeglasses removed, all sharp objects (pens, pencils) removed from their pockets. Then land as slowly as possible. By all means, if you have a shoulder harness, do it if possible. You may have seen race car drivers emerge unhurt from horrendous crashes at speeds in excess of 150 mph, because they were strapped in with seat belts and shoulder harnesses—and wore crash helmets.

Flaps and Gear

Every case is different, of course, but generally speaking the use of full flaps will produce the slowest landing speeds. There are, however, a couple of other aspects to the problem. First, the use of full flaps will steepen the glide appreciably, especially with a windmilling propeller situation, which is also all drag. Again, remember that unless you have actually landed your airplane with a windmilling (absolutely no power available) propeller, you do not know how the plane is going to fly and land in that configuration. This in turn sets up a very high—an abnormally high—sink-rate which is the cause of most spinal injuries and internal injuries in off-airport hard landings. Because the additional lift-producing camber of one or two notches of flap those settings will prevent the high sink-rate situation, but the full flap high-drag extension can be made at the last moment to knock off as much forward speed as possible.

By the same token, there are all kinds of arguments both ways as to whether retractible gear should be extended or left tucked away. One argument goes that if the gear is down, it will have the effect of tipping the plane over on its nose, but the counter-argument is that the gear is sufficiently fragile as far as a non-rolling, or "shear" condition is concerned, that it is best to leave it down and have the effect of its decelerative effect. My own inclination is to leave the gear down.

Landing On the Treetops

It is not always possible to find a flat area of ground on which to land, so that it may be necessary to land in a heavily wooded or forested area. Again, the slowest-controllable-airspeed landing advice still is valid and recommended, but there are some complications.

One does not have to fly to exotic places like the Matto Grosso, of darkest Africa or the Yucatan rain forest to learn that a heavy

Four occupants of this single engine lightplane escaped without injury when it shed parts landing in a wooded area. (Courtesy Penna. Bureau of Aviation)

forest will swallow up a downed airplane. One late fall not long ago I was involved with a Civil Air Patrol Search and Rescue mission, looking for a high-time but non-instrument-rated pilot who had taken off from a small airfield in Maine, headed for Nantucket Island, except that he disappeared somewhere en route. Because of a heavy fog in the New England region, the air search could not be started for three days, although we stood around the flight office at the local airport, drinking somewhat rancid coffee and plotting what we believed would have been the course he would have followed if he had been caught by the quick-forming fog. When the fog finally burned off, we put a gang of airplanes into the sky to scour the tree studded mountainsides for some indication of the lost plane. In two days of dawn to dusk, we found nothing. The hillside forests had simply swallowed him and his airplane. We were concerned because the report was that, as so many of us, he had jumped into his airplane wearing some lightweight clothing and carrying a load of fishing gear for snapper blues and striped bass. With no survival kit, he had no way of signalling and we had concluded that the battery of his impact-activated emergency locator transmitter (ELT) had become discharged while we were all stooging around waiting for the fog to lift.

By sheer good luck, our lost bird was found by a wilderness hiking group and taken back to the nearest community, some five miles away. He had, as he later reported, been forced down by clouds to a treetop level but realized that the temperature and dew

29

point were rapidly coming together which meant that pretty soon the air was going to become completely opaque, so rather than either spin in or out of control or hitting a mountain, he had elected to haul back on the throttle and land on the treetops only a few feet below. The landing, he reported, was a thing of beauty: a full stall that just kissed the tops of the trees, which cushioned and stopped the plane's forward progress, whereupon the plane slowly tipped over and fell straight down about 30 feet, with the result that the pilot broke his ankle and was unable to leave the wreck. For several days he had heard airplanes working up and down the valley but had been unable to signal them. If only—those terrible words!—if only he had had a smoke generator or a small personnel-type ELT, or a flare gun, he would have been found an hour after the air search had started. Wilderness survival? He was within a few miles of several communities. Fortunately for him, the surf fishing box contained two all metal thermos bottles, one of coffee and the other of good beef boullion. And that is why he came through it with only a bad cold to show for it.

Pick Your Best Spot

Once a pilot has recognized that the mathematical chances of completing the trip as planned are nil, whether because of a rough running engine or imminent fuel exhaustion because of horrendous headwinds, he has a priceless opportunity to make a reasoned judgment. Rather than simply blundering along until the fuel runs out and the airplane has to be put down wherever all power is lost, he has a choice. Whether it be over mountains, swamps, dense forests, arid desert or the briny deep, if he has as much as a half hour of fuel remaining, he can fly to a point 50 to 100 miles away, depending on the type and speed of his airplane. In most instances over North America this will enable him to proceed at least that much closer to civilization, calling for help on the radio distress frequency all the while to advise at least of his approximate position when he goes down. Fifty miles may not seem like much when you are roaring along on high—on some clear days, you can see that far from 1,500 feet—but if you consider the difficulty of surface travel in many types of terrain, so that it is frequently hard to cover one or two miles an hour on foot, climbing mountains or hacking your way through dense undergrowth, the time savings to transit a "mere" 50 miles can shorten the distance that must be walked appreciably: as much as a week, or more.

There is another aspect to anticipating an in-flight problem and taking action promptly: frequently one can select a landing site

The pilot of this Beechcraft elected to land in an open space when he lost an engine. An aircraft down in the open is easier to find—and easier to camp near. Courtesy FAA

31

better suited to survival than offered by the immediate environs. It may be a matter of flying from an area of steep hills to a broad, flat-bottomed valley, or from densely forested terrain to a region of flat grassland, or from overhead a huge morass, such as Georgia's Dismal Swamp, to a beach area, or from over open ocean to an island, however remote.

Conclusions

The conclusion is that survivable landings can be made out of emergency situations that develop in flight, so that the occupants of lightplanes can reasonably expect to be rescued and returned to their homes. It is a matter of education and preparation to cope with the problems of survival in the wilderness, stranded for a short time period.

Survival is dependent upon three requirements:

(1) Getting down safely;
(2) having a search and rescue effort initiated, and
(3) surmounting the problems of temporary isolation in the wild.

This is, of course, the basic theme of the book therefore, let me state the assumptions we began with, so that the survival and discovery sections will fall into place a bit more easily.

The first assumption is that we/you will have set up an alerting mechanism. The second assumption is that weather conditions will be such that a visual search and rescue effort can be in operation within two or three days at the most, which means discovery within a week, although we plan for a two week stay at the accident site. The third assumption is that we/you will have a survival plan set in mind and an adequate survival kit to carry it through. We will defer discussing the first assumption until later.

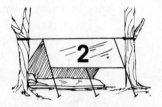

An Overview of Survival Problems

Before getting into the specifics of survival requirements, technique and equipment, let's take a look at the general requirements of "survival" in its broadest terms, including our normal day-to-day living back home.

Requirements for Survival

To survive *anywhere*, one must provide four basic human needs: water, shelter, fire and food, in about that order of importance. If any *two* of these are eliminated, the result is apt to be fatal, but if you can satisfy all four, the odds are strong that you will survive in good shape.

- *Water* is normally considered to be the most important bodily requirement for survival, with the possible change of priority under conditions of extreme cold where it is imperative that one's body-heat loss be prevented immediately or reduced as far as possible, either by insulating clothing or by a heat source, such as a large fire. Although most of us can live without food for as long as a couple of weeks, it is impossible to keep the human body functioning for more than a few days without water.
- *Shelter* entails more than a simple windbreak, if it is to be needed for more than a few hours. When we talk about shelter, it must be stressed that what we are really discussing is a sheltered place to *sleep*, because the ability to get a good night's sleep in comfort is—next to water—the most

important aspect to extended wilderness survival. Yet, the significance of sleep as an important function of our vital processes is lightly treated in most survival manuals. Without sleep, one's mind will not function efficiently, it becomes difficult to make decisions and to carry them out. With the loss of energy one's entire metabolic balance is upset and the normal levels of resistance to respiratory infections drops, so that it is not only possible but probably that one may be stricken with a debilitating illness.

As a result, "Shelter" therefore includes tents, ground cloths, sleeping bags and adequate clothing. Anything and everything that will literally protect your skin—which is *itself* a vital organ—from the elements and the creatures of nature.

• *Fire* has several functions, ranging from meeting the psychological need and for cooking, to signalling. In our view, the greatest need is the first one mentioned, for we have recognized the lenative effects of a roaring fire in the fireplace, whether at a campsite or in our own hearth. Fire is taken for granted by most people in these days of "cricket-type" lighters and available-almost-anywhere paper matches, but knowing how to start a fire in inclement weather in the open and especially keeping it going is beyond the skills of people whose idea of camping out is late night drinking on the patio. Yet this skill is vital to survival away from the trappings of modern civilization and we are going to spend some time discussing it later.

• *Food* is listed last because we can, if we have water, survive for a long time without it, living off our own fat. But it is an uncomfortable, frequently physically painful situation and of course food is a necessity if one is to operate at full strength and efficiency. Although an inactive person can survive for weeks with no solid food, it is obvious that one's normal caloric burn-off created by physical activity, such as chopping wood to keep a fire going, must be replaced—at least partially—if an active pace is to be maintained for long.

The Fear of the Unknown

A severe problem which must be anticipated is the mental state of anyone not versed in woodsmanship, evidenced by a mounting sensation of isolation and helplessness, plus the innate fear of the unknown, which is the city dweller's reaction to being displaced into the wilderness. Separately and certainly together, these psychologi-

34

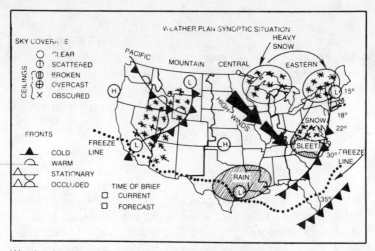

Weather in the middle of winter can be bad enough to require cold weather survival equipment all over the United States. Note that freezing conditions existed everywhere except in Southern California and along the US-Mexican Border. On this date, there was snow in Las Vegas, Phoenix, and Palm Springs. Miami was a scant three degrees above freezing. Date was 2 February, 1979.

cal quirks create an effective barrier to thought processes and the abilities to plan and act. Therefore, just as—and for the same reasons—many of us who regularly fly twin engine aircraft take recurrent refresher courses in coping with abnormal flight situations, it is important for everyone to design and occasionally to review and assess a plan of action for wilderness sojourns, before the need arises. Although the situation and the need for such a plan may never arise, it is worthwhile to remember an old Western cowboy saying to the effect that, "You may carry a gun for years and not need it. But when you *do* need it, you need it damn badly and the biggest gun is none too big". So it is with advance planning for wilderness survival and creating survival kits. Just read the old cowboy saying quoted above, and substitute "survival kit" for "gun", because having a plan is not enough. You also need the equipment to carry it out.

About First Aid

To be perfectly candid, a course in First Aid, except for a few basics and generalities, is beyond the scope of this book. For an excellent dissertation on various techniques of resuscitation, the locations of pressure points to stem arterial bleeding, handling heart attacks and choking seizures, the best manual around is the American Red Cross publication *First Aid and Personal Safety*, obtainable from the ARC, Washington, D.C. However, I must say that having the book is not enough; recognizing the hazards of living in modern society everyone, pilot or not, owes it to himself/herself and their family to take a good First Aid course every year. Most high school extension course programs make such courses available.

Notwithstanding that forced landings off airports, if carried out at the slowest possible *controllable* airspeed and least sink-rate, result in minimal injuries, if the occupants and all luggage is properly restrained, the pilot—the captain—must be prepared to administer treatment for injuries, illnesses, or both. This means having an adequate First Aid kit in the airplane, complete with pressure bandages, gauze bandages, surgical adhesive tape, absorbent cotton, cotton swabs, merthiolate, aspirin, sunburn ointment, ammonia ampules and band-aids. Good first aid kits are available from pharmaceutical houses and from boating and aviation supply houses, such as Sporty's in Cincinnatti, Ohio. Many large marinas and fixed base operations also sell them. Over the years, we have made up our own which is carried in a metal box $8'' \times 9\frac{1}{2}'' \times 2\frac{1}{2}''$ which is affixed by a quick-detach mount on the rear bulkhead and contains everything except large splints. We have used it a number of times in the past. The worst was when a passenger misjudged the distance from the wing of our Apache to the ground, missed the fixed step and fell, cutting a deep gash in his shin. We fixed him up then took him to the hospital to be sewed back together. (The local newspaper headlined it, "Foreign Visitor Injured in Aircraft Accident".) Another time, I stepped on a sea urchin in the Bahamas while skinny-dipping from an airstrip-side beach. My advice is: Don't do it.

A word about storing such kits, or for that matter any small objects. From time to time we see such items lying on the rear shelves—the "hat shelves"—of friends' airplanes, a practice which I must caution against, for it can have a lethal effect if the airplane comes to a sudden stop.

Several years ago a good friend was forced to ditch at sea. Having alerted the FAA of his descent, the Coast Guard plucked him from the bosom of the sea before his fingers wrinkled, so he had no problems, but he was really impressed by one facet of the incident: his passenger had laid a little all-wave battery-powered portable radio on the rear shelf, weighing not more than a couple of pounds. When the plane skipped off the top of the first wave only to hit the second wave head-on, which stopped it cold, the little radio kept going at the rate of 60 mph, which translates to about 90 feet a second, zipped between the occupants' heads and cut a neat oblong

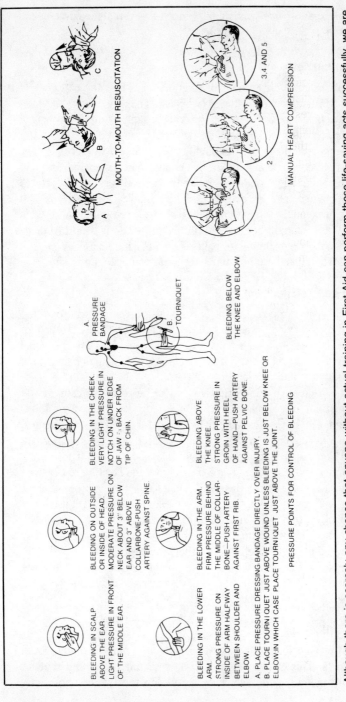

BLEEDING IN SCALP ABOVE THE EAR. LIGHT PRESSURE IN FRONT OF THE MIDDLE EAR.

BLEEDING ON OUTSIDE OR INSIDE OF HEAD. MODERATE PRESSURE ON NECK ABOUT 3" BELOW EAR AND 3" ABOVE COLLARBONE-PUSH ARTERY AGAINST SPINE.

BLEEDING IN THE CHEEK. VERY LIGHT PRESSURE IN NOTCH ON UNDER EDGE OF JAW ⅔ BACK FROM TIP OF CHIN.

BLEEDING IN THE LOWER ARM. STRONG PRESSURE ON INSIDE OF ARM HALFWAY BETWEEN SHOULDER AND ELBOW.

BLEEDING IN THE ARM. FIRM PRESSURE BEHIND THE MIDDLE OF COLLAR- BONE—PUSH ARTERY AGAINST FIRST RIB

BLEEDING ABOVE THE KNEE. STRONG PRESSURE IN GROIN WITH HEEL OF HAND—PUSH ARTERY AGAINST PELVIC BONE.

A. PLACE PRESSURE DRESSING BANDAGE DIRECTLY OVER INJURY.
B. PLACE TOURNIQUET JUST ABOVE WOUND UNLESS BLEEDING IS JUST BELOW KNEE OR ELBOW IN WHICH CASE PLACE TOURNIQUET JUST ABOVE THE JOINT

A PRESSURE BANDAGE
B TOURNIQUET

BLEEDING BELOW THE KNEE AND ELBOW

PRESSURE POINTS FOR CONTROL OF BLEEDING

MOUTH-TO-MOUTH RESUSCITATION

3, 4 AND 5

2

1

MANUAL HEART COMPRESSION

Although there is scarcely any chance that anyone without actual training in First Aid can perform these life-saving acts successfully, we are including, directly from the Air Force Survival Manual the following instructions on what to do if one of your companions is 1) bleeding badly, 2) has stopped breathing, or 3) has had a heart attack. From USAF Manual AFM-64-5

37

hole in the one-piece windshield. Since I heard that, we use the hat shelf of our airplane only for *hats*.

Typical Injuries

Most injuries from controlled crashes fall into the category of cuts and bruises, muscle strains (whiplash) and dislocations. If a high sink rate is allowed to develop, aircraft occupants may have spinal injuries, or internal injuries, particularly if physically soft. If the airplane comes down hard enough to produce any fractures, sever sprains or concussions, unless you have had extensive first aid training, about all you can do is make the injured person comfortable and let nature take its course until real medical help arrives. No matter how much training you may have had, remember first aid is about 90% common sense. The first thing to do is stop bleeding, dress wounds and administer pain killing medicine. In any event, the most serious problem you must face and comprehend is shock.

Shock and its Treatment

Shock is a medical term describing a physiological condition caused by injury or a mental jolt. It is characterized by trembling, cold sweats, thirst, a certain numbness of the mind (as if the personal experience is being viewed from afar), lack of feeling of pain from a serious injury and a felling of faintness or light-headedness. It is important that anyone suffering from shock be kept warm not only by clothing and coverings, but by warm drinks and warm food, although—to borrow a somewhat turgid line from the medical profession—alcoholic drinks are not indicated. The person in shock should have his/her head placed lower than his/her feet, if possible.

Shock can last as long as a day or two and is likely to be more severe in accordance with the extent of the person's physical injuries. It must be added that you, the pilot (particularly if it is your own airplane that is laying out there in a heap), will go into some degree of shock, if for no other reason than that you have lost your bird, so be mentally prepared for that, too. Remember, if you have planned for your survival, have developed the tough mental attitude and have landed under control, you will survive the wrecking of your airplane. You can always get another airplane, later.

Typical Illnesses

After any traumatic experience, anyone's innards tend to jump the tracks. This can be aggravated by ingesting the wrong kinds of food or drinking water, which can result in a form of food poisoning with such symptoms as upset stomach, complete with vomiting and diarrhea. These situations are far more serious medically than most laymen realize, for they are dehydrating; they actually pull water out of the body, which soon causes all sorts of problems with one's metabolism. Water—liquids—so lost must be replaced immediately, otherwise can have fatal consequences.

Water is an indispensable necessity for sustaining human life. Almost 80% of our body weight is water and if a physical imbalance of as little as 7% or 8% develops, there is not enough water to support vital bodily functions. Serious debilitation, quickly followed by incapacitation will result. And if the loss-of-liquid situation is not reversed and a normal balance restored, death will follow. Dehydration is a very serious situation, which must be guarded against, particularly in survival situations, where water may be limited in the first place.

To give you an idea of the dimensions of the water requirement for an adult human being, consider this: under ordinary circumstances, a moderately active adult will transpire—go through—about three *quarts* of water a day. About half of that will be passed as urine and other bodily metabolic wastes. Approximately another quart will be exhuded by one's lungs in the normal course of respiration in which cool air is inhaled, warmed within the lungs and thereby humidified, then exhaled. In summertime the lost moisture is invisible, but in wintertime the warm, moisture-laden air is cooled and condensed, so you can see your breath. And normally about a pint of liquid will be lost by perspiration in the natural function of cooling the body by skin surface evaporation to maintain the normal temperature of 98.6°F.

This normal water loss due to transpiration must be balanced by an equivalent water intake to maintain the vital required level and it is clear that any physical exercise or extremely hot weather, both of which will raise the body's self-regulated core temperature, will in turn bring about a reaction from the cooling organ known as the skin, which will exude perspiration to dissipate heat by evaporative cooling, which increases the need for a corresponding amount of water intake. Conversely, in cold weather the skin's perspiration producing pores shut down tight as the body acts to contain its heat, so that water loss is reduced.

It can be seen then, that the possibility of survival can be seriously reduced by dehydration and the reason for the terrible potential of diarrhea and nausea, both of which create immediate and severe—physicians use the term, "dramatic"—water imbalance which requires immediate replacement of literally gallons of water as quickly as possible. A victim of food poisoning requires hospitalization and even then it can be touch-and-go, which is why I am not inclined to eat wild berries and tree roots.

Aside from those abnormal causes of dehydration, maintaining a normal liquid balance in the body requires equalizing the liquid intake and pass-out, so that if your water *supply* is limited the best way to conserve it and stay healthy is to control the amount you *lose*; if you reduce the amount you pass in urine, perspiration and heavy breathing, not as much water will have to be replaced. This means that, if there is not much water available, you must plan to take it easy and not to work too hard or too fast. It is a commonly held misapprehension that one can continue to function longer simply by rationing the available water supply. The real fact is that water rationing, without water loss conservation, merely creates a pattern of creeping debilitation.

With those preliminaries, let's get into the issues of practical survival practices after the fall.

Setting up Housekeeping, Basic Instructions

O.K., so here we are on the ground, hands on hips, looking at the bent airplane, wondering, "What do I do now?"

At this point, I must confess to being irked by survival writers who recommend that a pilot, after he crawls out of the wreck of his beautiful airplane and all of the associated thought processes involved in such an experience, must remain calm. Having been through such a crunch myself, I can say that under those circumstances a pilot will probably be as upset as he has ever been—or ever will be—in his entire life. It is important to keep in mind that you will probably go into at least a light form of "shock" as a result of the entire experience, which will result in a certain unreal, dreamlike reaction to what is going on, a perfectly natural, predictable reaction.

Because of this, you should consider having a few basic instructions of what *not* to do written down, possibly laminated in plastic, like this:

Forced Landings Off-Airports
1. Do NOT overdo physical activity.
2. Do NOT allow yourself to become overtired or exhausted.
3. Do NOT move around too fast—Watch your step!
4. Do NOT stray from the aircraft and become lost (or allow anyone else to leave the vicinity!)
5. Prepare to set up a survival camp.

This may sound pretty elementary, but remember that you will be operating in a mental fog and it helps to have some mental crutches to get you back on the track again.

First Things First

The first step in your mental preparation, to make it almost an automatic, reflexive action, is to plan to get out of the airplane as quickly as possible as soon as it comes to a stop and to take a basic survival kit with you, including at least one canteen of water. Then, linger for a while far enough from the airplane that you are sure that there will be no fire from spilled fuel. Fortunately, there are not many post-landing fires in the recorded cases, but it pays to be careful.

A safe distance away from the wreck—particularly if fuel is leaking—clear a small area not overhung with dead trees (from which limbs may fall and rain and snow will surely drip), set up a preliminary shelter and build the makin's of a campfire large enough to provide some heat and light and to prepare some hot drinks or food. A campfire is almost mandatory if the temperature is cold for it will be necessary to offset excess body-heat loss due to shock. Nutritionists suggest that hot chocolate is better for this purpose than either coffee or tea, both of which contain caffein. Then, set up your emergency locator transmitter (ELT), but *don't turn it on yet*; wait until you see or hear aircraft in the vicinity. It does not make sense to drain the power of the ELT battery on "blind transmissions", particularly if it may take a few days to get the search program into action. It certainly would be tragic if the ELT was dead when airplanes were within 20 miles. But, be prepared to activate the ELT the moment any aircraft are seen or heard. And have someone looking for them as much as possible, particularly in hours of daylight when most searches are carried out.

Then, set up your other signalling devices, which we will discuss in detail later, and prepare signalling fires to make smoke plumes. And don't forget to check the wrecked airplane to see if the lead-acid battery is still providing sufficient current to operate the radios and switch your transceivers on and off to see if they are operable. Usually, they are. I was involved in a rescue in New England where a Cessna 140 landed upside down in a dense forest—actually, the pilot flared out just above the treetops, settled in and slowly slid to the ground shedding wings and things along the way and wound up inverted on the carpet of pine needles. He was located two days later, hungry but well, having directed the aircraft circling overhead by his airplane's radio, although the searchers could not see the silvery little plane: the trees had opened up, engulfed it and closed together, thereby hiding it. I might add that this was before the days of ELTs.

The main thing is that, for a couple of hours after the landing, instead of sitting around wondering what will become of you, you will be *doing something*!! That is the best treatment for the shock syndrome. Then, once the first burst of nervous energy has been expended, it is important that you be able to lie down and get some rest and keep warm until all shock symptoms from the disaster wear off.

You might as well sleep all night, particularly that first night, because the strong odds are that no one is going to come looking for you after the sun goes down, anyhow.

The Basic Survival Kit

A basic survival kit is really designed to support two people for two days in warm weather situations. It provides only minimal equipment and should not be relied on for a lengthy stay, even under the best of conditions. Several companies make emergency survival kits of various sizes, from one-person models costing in the neighborhood of $5 to large two and four-person versions costing up to $125. The smaller ones come in pocket-sized packets (5″ × 6″ plastic bags), medium, two-person kits sold commercially come in containers approximately 4″ × 6″ × 8″, weighing around three pounds each and the big, four-person type comes in a two-handled cylindrical tote bag about a foot in diameter and a foot and a half long—a bit over one cubic foot of space.

Commercial Basic Survival Kits

Survival kits of many types are available over the counter, ranging from small ones some of which are wholly contained in a small cylindrical carrier about two inches in diameter and six inches long. One of these is known as the Pac-Kit™ available from Eddie Bauer; another is the Nicolet "Mini Survival Kit" which is contained in a little plastic baggy, about 5″ × 6″. Both of these little kits can be carried in a coat pocket or in the glove or side pockets of lightplanes.

However, look out for weasel-wording in advertisements and don't be afraid to examine the contents of a kit you may be contemplating. Not long ago I picked up a commercially available kit advertised as "containing more than 50 items that could help save the life" of an airman down in the brush. In it I found a container of ordinary cardboard or paper matches, a six inch long candle about ¾ inch in diameter, six small balls of absorbent cotton ("tinder"), a cheap plastic "police-type" whistle, four boullion cubes and a military-type hand held can opener.

Some commercial kits come in large packages which will, according to the manufacturers, sustain four people for several days under all but the worst conditions of weather and climate. The larger kits contain waterproof matches, small candles, fishing line, hooks and some emergency food rations as well as really basic first aid materials: adhesive bandages, burn ointments, mosquito repellent, etc. However, the smaller kits are bare minimum kits, at best. No commercial survival kit includes provisions for water. We will get to that problem a little later.

The most popular kits commercially available are larger than the pocket-sized "mini kits" but small enough to be carried on one's belt in the manner of a canteen and provide for *basic* survival requirements in mild climate conditions. Typical of this class are the Nicolet "Survivor I" and the survival kit of the Aircraft Owners and Pilots Association (AOPA) and the AOPA Air Safety Foundation. Both kits are comparable in both size and contents, but I know the AOPA kit best, since I have one.

The AOPA survival kit, contained in a light canvas bag, 6″ × 4″ × 9″ and weighing in at about three pounds (complete with a belt loop) contains the following:

For Shelter: a tube tent of blaze orange plastic, 2 space blankets

For Fire: a fire starter kit including several strike-anywhere wooden matches, several small clumps of tinder material, a plumber's candle, four fuel tablets, a metal spark striker (permanent match), a magnifying glass (burning glass)

For Signalling: a plastic (police-type) whistle, a signalling mirror (4″ × 4″), 3 seven-second flares

For First Aid: insect repellent in tube, water purification tablets, adhesive strip bandages, burn ointment, antacid tablets

Miscellaneous: several safety pins, pen knife (3″ blade), pair of pliers, file, 10 feet of copper wire, flexible (wire) saw, (1) razor blade and a small hand held compass and 4 sheets of toilet tissue

Food: 4 packets Hershey's hot cocoa mix, several freeze dried chicken soup packets, Pillsbury emergency food sticks, 2 small aluminum foil cups, 5 fishhooks, 50′ of nylon line, 4 split shot

And several booklets on survival in the wilderness.

The AOPA/Nicolet type of basic one-person survival kit is, however, just that: basic. If one assumes that he is going to be uncomfortable physically after a forced landing in the wilderness, and will be hungry, wet and cold—and thirsty—but will survive anyhow, these easily stored portable basic kits will be good enough. It all gets back to the psychological situation affecting a pilot who is faced with the possibility of descending into a wilderness survival situation: if he is totally unequipped and unprepared to cope with such a situation, he may attempt to fly back to civilization, no matter what, pushing until the tanks run dry or the power is otherwise totally lost and he will have no alternative except to make what we all must recognize as the most hazardous type of landing, without power, completely dead-stick. However, if the same pilot has both survival equipment and the knowledge to use it, so that he does feel that he will be able to survive the experience—even though the airplane may be thereby rendered null and void—he may be able to make a non-pressurized judgment, rather than cave into panic. He may calmly (or not so calmly!) elect to put down while he still controls the situation. Hence, even a basic survival kit may have a salutory effect on the decisional process. And as the saying goes, *something* is better than *nothing*.

A year or two ago, AOPA introduced a survival course for its members as part of the association's series of pilot-upgrading courses regularly presented all over the country. When the survival course was initiated, no one had any idea of the degree of interest, if any, that might be shown. After all, there is some negative aspect to the whole idea of a survival program, since it begins with an aircraft accident.

Somewhat to everyones' amazement the course was immediately and overwhelmingly accepted (and usually oversubscribed) which required an immediate expansion of the presentation. Originally designed around a series of classroom lectures and demonstrations, the real problems of survival were made clear when the training syllabus was extended to include a day in the field after the classroom demonstration, so that the students had to go through all the drills of a simulated forced landing, including fire-making, shelter construction, basic first aid, locating sources of fresh water and obtaining food. Within a year, the course was further expanded to include an overnight in the "wilds," with the trainees being required to use only equipment provided by their AOPA survival kits.

It did not take long to learn that the old-style survival courses of make-do-with-what-you-have—using a watch crystal filled with

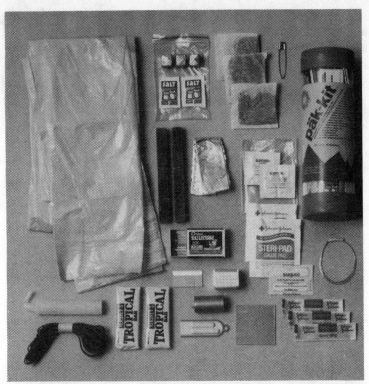

The Pak-Kit pocket-sized survival kit is designed for hunters, hikers, skiers and others who may find themselves lost and overcome by darkness. This compact kit, in a waterproof 8½-in × 2-¾-in tube, contains a tube tent, signal mirror, whistle, basic first aid supplies, candle, flaresticks, waterproof matches, nylon cord, wire, duct tape, razor blade, aluminum foil, dextrose cubes, energy bars, salt packets, bouillon cubes, tea bags, and waterproof cards with instructions for first aid, fire building, shelter, weather-travel, and hypothermia. Courtesy Eddie Bauer, Inc.

water as a magnifying glass to start a fire; using one's shoelaces to make snares to catch small game; flint, steel and tinder fire starters; ripping out upholstery and carpeting to make bedding—were (and are) last-ditch techniques and that the time to become educated is before such knowledge may amount to a matter of life, or death.

I must repeat that, as far as the inclusion of a "how-to" book on selecting plant life for inclusion in one's diet when downed in the bush is concerned, it is little short of a fraud on the victim of circumstances. I have used several such illustrative manuals which contain black and white line drawings of edible and poisonous plants while on jaunts afield and have never been able to identify any of the plants set forth with enough assurance that I was not going to wind up with gastronomical difficulties and possibly worse. Merely including such information in a survival manual seems to serve no really useful purpose and when we began to become personally involved in preparing for survival, we decided to eliminate such illustrations and take a different tack. We cannot believe that anyone can be expected to survive on the basis of on-the-job (or at-the-crash-site)—a crash course?—training from a book.

Our Grab Bag Survival Kit

Over the years we have accumulated all sorts of airline carrying bags and similar bags available from various lightplane manufacturers, so we pulled a couple out of the hall closet and began to work up a basic survival kit of our own, one that would fit our specific needs and cover any possible inadequacies as woodsmen.

We chose two types of bag. The first (courtesy of Delta Air Lines) was a top-zipper closure bag with a pair of handles measuring 15″ × 6½″ at the base and about 9½″ high. The second, acquired from Piper Aircraft Corp., measured 4¼″ × 10″ × 13½″. The Delta bag, at 926¼ cubic inch was about half again as large in content as the Piper bag, at 573¾ cubic inch (My wife countered by saying that we could use *two* Piper bags). We were in agreement that this would be a basic "fair weather" survival kit, really usable only when the nighttime temperatures did not plunge below the freezing level under circumstances where we had to spend a couple of nights in the out of doors. In other words, late spring, summer and early fall weather characteristically encountered in the Middle Atlantic region.

The AOPA Survival Kit, left above, is a basic kit. Our home made survival kit—the "Grab Bag"—is contained in the airline bag.

We started with the smaller bag, from Piper, which had more than twice the cubic content than the AOPA bag (216 cubic inch), to see how it would work out. The Delta bag was held in reserve.

Our priorities were, as you would expect water, shelter, fire and food. Our basic *water supply* was set into two quart-sized surplus military canteens in their own cloth containers with their canteen cups. For *shelter*, we packed in a well folded pair of lightweight military surplus nylon ponchos and two sets of fishnet underwear and two nylon shell windbreakers. For *fire* we added several containers of carefully prepared waterproofed strike anywhere kitchen matches and a sharp knife to prepare tinder (fuzz sticks), plus a hatchet. For *food*, we started with packets of dehydrated and freeze-dried foods available in most supermarkets and outdoors supplies stores. By the time we got through, the little Piper bag was more than full, including all of the above, plus:

A "personnel-type" ELT (as a back-up to the airplane's)
Signalling mirrors (2)
Brass police whistles (2)
Orange-smoke signal generators (6)
Two plumbers' candles
A bottle of water purification tablets
Extra socks and underwear
50' of light nylon rope
Sunburn block and insect repellent (1 tube each)
2 antimosquito headnets
One week's supply of freeze-dried food in packets
Several squares of heavy aluminum foil (4" × 4", opening up to 12" × 16")
Tweezers and safety pins in a sewing kit (with buttons)
Several pocket-sized packs of Kleenex (for toilet paper)
A pair of needle-nosed pliers with side cutters.
A dozen nails
A container of heat-tablets and a little stove that can be folded to fit into a pocket
A collapsable Sterno stove and two cans of Sterno
and
A basic first aid kit containing:
       Darvan pain-killing pills
       Band-aids
       adhesive tape
       absorbent cotton
       pair of scissors (4")
       bottle of salt tablets

compression bandages
a plastic bottle of aspirin
a plastic bottle of vitamin pills
a plastic bottle of brewer's yeast
a plastic bottle of vibramyacin for diarrhea

Obviously, we turned to the Delta bag because it was needed.

With the contents of our "grab bag"—properly, our "grab-it-and-get-out bag"—we should be able to last a few days if the weather is on the warm side, particularly if we can make use of the clothing in our luggage and the extra equipment usually stashed away in the airplane. But this is only a fair weather stop-gap. If we expect to survive under any but the most optimum conditions, we know that we have to have more than our grab-bag can supply.

Commercial Survival Kits for Heavy Going

The largest commercial survival kit with which we have any personal experience is made by Nicolet Products in Phoenix, Arizona and was specially designed for light aircraft applications, with an eye to compactness, light weight and expense. Their largest model, called the Survivor IV contains a number of items including 18 packets each of reconstitutable chicken-type soup, and beef soup, hot chocolate mix, two dozen small tropical (i.e.: won't melt in the heat) chocolate bars, high-energy trail foods, cookies and water-must-be-added beverages. The Survivor IV also has police whistles, a signalling mirror (although not the military type), a first aid kit, fire starter kit, four aluminized space blankets and two two-person tube tents. This kit, according to our calculations has shelter for four people for three days. It has been tested in the field by a number of experienced campers and outdoorsmen and has been improved over the years. It is available through Sporty's aviation-oriented mail order house in Cincinnati, Ohio.

However . . . . .

Since we got on this survival kick, we have begun to evolve a more personal survival kit, tailored for the worst, not the best conditions. There was a personal reason for this. In the last two years, we lost friends who made uneventful landings in winter, apparently precautionary landings because of deteriorating weather, then froze to death in the cabins of their undamaged airplanes. What we wanted was a survival kit that would make it possible for us to win that battle with Mother Nature.

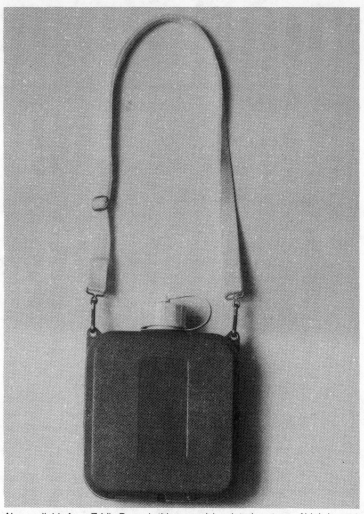

Also available from Eddie Bauer is this rugged, insulated canteen of high-impact plastic. It will keep one quart of liquid hot or cold up to five hours. It also floats.

Whether you agree with the size or contents of our large survival kit, or think it is excessive for your own needs, let me tell you why we developed it as we have. Then, you can make up your own mind.

Compromises, Compromises

Whenever anyone designs anything where any constraints are imposed, whether they be financial, size or weight, there must be

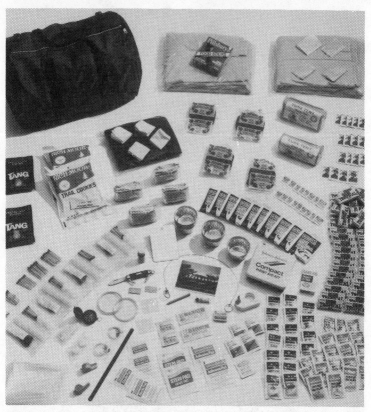

An excellent commercially available survival kit by Nicolet Products is available from Sporty's (Sportsmans Market, Aviation Division, Clermont County Airport, Batavia, Ohio) is 12 × 17 inches, 15 lbs, designed for four people for a minimum of four days and has a storage life of five years.

some trade-offs, some compromises. But our objective is to create a survival package that will enable us to come out of a week or ten days in the wilderness which meant it would have to provide the four requirements to sustain human life. We started by brainstorming, selecting equipment without restraint, but realized that to furnish everything we wanted would have required the cubic contents of a Boeing 747, instead of a portable bag in the cabin of a lightplane. Then with a bit of fudging and allowances for the kind of clothing we would be normally wearing under the circumstances, we believe we came up with it.

Before we get into the contents, however, let's analyze the basic requirements for survival generally conceded by all authorities on the subject to be necessary as essentials to survival for human beings.

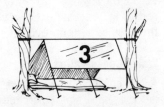

Meeting the First
Requirement: Water

Those of us who live in so-called civilized communities, where a room can be flooded with light at the click of a switch, indoors temperatures can be regulated automatically with thermostats that activate air conditioners or heaters, and water that flows at the turn of a tap, take water for granted. Few people are aware of the utter dependence our lives have on water. The hard fact is that, unless you have an unlimited supply of water available for drinking purposes, your very life is in danger. Therefore, if you are downed in the wilderness and have to depend entirely on what water you carry with you, you will be in serious trouble within a few days.

The Need for Water

It can be seen then that the possibility of survival is seriously reduced by dehydration and the potentially lethal effects of both nausea and diarrhea can be understood, for both of these conditions create severe and dramatic dehydration imbalance which requires the immediate replacement of literally gallons of water. This is why I do not believe in relying at all on indigenous nuts, berries or tree roots for survival. At best, they can taste bad. At worst, they can dehydrate you by upsetting your digestive system. If you still don't believe how deadly serious this is, ask a physician about the treatment for food poisoning—even if it is contracted at the best restaurant in town.

Putting the daily requirement of three pints of water a day into perspective that most of us can visualize: it is the equivalent of six full (eight ounce) drinking glasses a day of water in some form. It may be in tea, cocoa, soup, or in fresh fruit—or for that matter in beer or wine, just so it is liquid containing mostly water. Six such glasses a day comes out to slightly more than one-third of a gallon requirement for *each* occupant of the aircraft. If two people are on board they will consume three-quarters of a gallon a day and five gallons should suffice for a week—if they are not engaged in heavy physical work and/or in hot climate. However, if you have four or more people in the downed aircraft, even five gallons is not going to last very long.

Water Conservation

When it comes to conserving water, most of us think in terms of rationing small sips to parched lips, something we might have seen in old movies about ship sinkings on the high seas. However, the medical recommendation of all survival experts is that maintaining normal liquid balance in the body requires equalizing the liquid in-take and pass-out principally by controlling ("rationing", if you will) the amount you *lose*, rather than by conserving it by rationing its consumption. By conserving energy, perspiration, heavy breathing and urination, not as much water must be replaced. This means that you must plan to take it easy and not work too hard or too fast, unless you have an unlimited supply of drinking water near at hand.

Water Availability

As I keep repeating, since no commercially available survival kit has any provisions for water, which is *the* essential for a prolonged stay anywhere, if your planning includes a half gallon of water for *each* person in the airplane, you should be pretty well set for a day and a half of normal intake level of six glasses of water (or liquid) a day. But once you have set up camp, built a pyre of wood for your cooking and smoke-making fires and arranged your signalling equipment, you must begin looking for other sources of water.

Generally, wherever you find forests, you will also find fresh water in streams, ponds and lakes, most of which will be drinkable as you find it. However, no matter how clear they may look, most outdoors writers recommend that *all* water be purified for drinking either by treating it chemically or by boiling. Commercial preparations, iodine or halazone tablets are available for chemical purification from most pharmacists.

In winter, when there is snow on the ground, one only has to melt it down in a pot or piece of aluminum foil shaped like a dish, over the open fire, although it is amazing how much snow it takes to make

	MAXIMUM DAILY TEMPERATURE (°F) IN SHADE ▼	AVAILABLE WATER PER MAN, U.S. QUARTS					
		0	1 Qt	2 Qts	4 Qts	10 Qts	20 Qts
NO WALKING AT ALL		DAYS OF EXPECTED SURVIVAL					
	120°	2	2	2	2.5	3	4.5
	110	3	3	3.5	4	5	7
	100	5	5.5	6	7	9.5	13.5
	90	7	8	9	10.5	15	23
	80	9	10	11	13	19	29
	70	10	11	12	14	20.5	32
	60	10	11	12	14	21	32
	50	10	11	12	14.5	21	32

	MAXIMUM DAILY TEMPERATURE (°F) IN SHADE ▼	AVAILABLE WATER PER MAN, U.S. QUARTS					
		0	1 Qt	2 Qts	4 Qts	10 Qts	20 Qts
WALKING AT NIGHT UNTIL EXHAUSTED AND RESTING THEREAFTER		DAYS OF EXPECTED SURVIVAL					
	120°	1	2	2	2.5	3	
	110	2	2	2.5	3	3.5	
	100	3	3.5	3.5	4.5	5.5	
	90	5	5.5	5.5	6.5	8	
	80	7	7.5	8	9.5	11.5	
	70	7.5	8	9	10.5	13.5	
	60	8	8.5	9	11	14	
	50	8	8.5	9	11	14	

Days of expected survival in the desert under two conditions.

one small basin of water. If it is extremely cold, you can have some real problems keeping water liquid, no matter what its source, for it can freeze solid in a matter of hours—sometimes, minutes. Worse, if it is in a container, such as a canteen or jug, the water expands as it freezes and will rupture the container, making it useless for the purpose in the future. It is better to let it freeze in shallow, open containers, for it can then be remelted. Heavy duty aluminum foil is ideal for this situation.

Strangely enough, there are many streams and waterfalls in the mountains, frequently spewing out of what appears to be solid rock.

Water in the Desert

For all practical purposes, there is no water in a desert, so the best advice is to carry as much with you as possible. I will say that my realization of the water problem has changed my routings across the western United States so that we stay reasonably close to the Interstate Highways. All it took was a close view of the bleaching bones of a few head of cattle out there on the dry, dusty plain.

Just about all survival texts contain instructions for building what are called "solar stills" so that airmen down on the desert can obtain drinkable water. I have included it here, although truthfully, I have never been able to make one work the way the manuals say it should.

The theory of the solar still is that radiant heat from the sun will create high temperatures within a hole in the ground covered by a clear plastic sheet. The super-heated air will then absorb moisture and produce a high humidity condition in the cavity beneath the plastic, which will become cooled where it touches the sheet, thus turns into "dew" which in turn drips down the inner surface of the plastic into a container placed at the bottom of the hole in the ground, and Voila! Drinkable water.

That's the theory. In practice, it must be understood that, to begin with, there must be a source of moisture to be vaporized, such as urine, tainted water (preferably soaked in sponges) or moisture-laden plants. Moreover, most survival texts admit that each solar still will under optimum conditions produce only a half pint of water in 24 hours, far below the normal human three quart requirement. This means that at least twelve solar stills would be required to fill the needs of *each* occupant of the downed aircraft, if he or she is to survive.

Aside from the unavailability of a dozen clear 6′ × 6′ plastic sheets for each person and—except for landings on deserted islands—the unavailability of moisture or moisture-containing material to "prime" the solar stills, and discounting the amount of moisture that the still's interior would itself absorb, the expenditure of energy in digging the holes for the stills and constructing them would surely result in a far greater loss—through transpiration—than could ever be made up. Therefore, we recommend that if you go down in the desert, the first thing to do is rig up some sun shades, then keep out of the sun and any breeze and the second thing is to do as little as possible: don't work, don't walk and don't sweat.

Desert Water Sources

Hot weather survival is almost as difficult as cold weather survival if for no other reason than that the human body's metabolism has to undergo such a change to adapt to it. Survival in the desert, where less than six inches of total rainfall may drop in an entire year, also requires a greater than normal amount of water because of losses due to transpiration. In the desert areas of the Southwest and parts of Mexico the best source of moisture is the barrel cactus which retains water for a long time after absorbing it from one of those rare showers. The plant is well named. Not only is it shaped roughly like a barrel, it has a very hard rind about as tough as a barrel and protected by sharp spines, a second cousin to barbed wire. But if you have a heavy knife or an axe, you can cut through the tough outer layer and reach the somewhat pulpy water-soaked insides which can

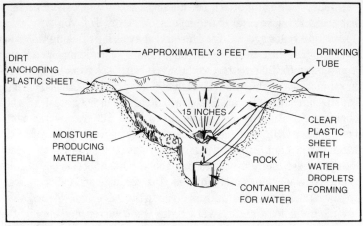

Solar still.

be used to "prime" the solar stills discussed above, if you are so inclined and have the requisite plastic ground cloths. In addition, the pulp can be cut out in chunks and chewed to extract the moisture, producing a residue that is fibrous and ill-tasting. But, there is some moisture available.

There are also some water holes in the desert. Whenever you are flying across an arid area, keep your eyes peeled for spots of green which indicate moisture on or near to the surface, for all bushes and trees require water. Although we plan to follow well travelled highways across the wide open spaces, there have been times when we traversed places that looked as barren and inhospitable as the face of the moon, as when flying from Mazatlan to Matamoros, in Mexico or down the length of the Baja California peninsula.

About the only nice thing anyone can say about going down in a desert area is that the air is generally so clear and cloudless that visual signalling devices can be seen for a long way, especially reflections of the sun by a signalling mirror and smoke columns, either chemically generated or from oil, gasoline and fabric from the downed airplane. And at night a flashlight or strobe light can be seen against the velvet blackness of the desert from miles above. We will get to the use of signalling equipment later.

Portable and Potable

In our two survival kits, the "grab bag" and our larger bag, which we will describe fully when we finish with the requirements for survival, we carry four one-quart canteens of fresh water with which we believe we can get out of the airplane very quickly. We also habitually carry several extra gallons of water. Tell you why.

Many years ago we discovered that available drinking water at many of the places we went as tourists, vacationers, conventioneers, or for that matter, for business purposes, was—no matter how much of it gushed from the faucet—flat and tasteless and what it (or ice cubes made from it) did to a scotch, rye or sour mash was an abomination. As a result, we began to airlift our own water from Ocean City, N.J., which is a pure and tangy as water from a Rocky Mountain stream. At first we used old glass bottles, but soon found that the best method was to use those nifty unbreakable plastic bottles now used so widely for milk, orange juice and cider; at first we used the quart size, then moved up to the half gallon size and now use the full gallons, since several times when we reached our night's perch, tossed out the ice cubes in the little refrigerator and whipped up a batch of social nostrums with the airlifted aqua pura, we received so many requests for both our water and ice that out of the necessity of protecting our own palates we began to carry as much as four or five gallons at a time in our luggage compartment—about 40 pounds worth—firmly secured by a cargo net. We did it for fun, not thinking of survival of the type we are discussing in this book. It wasn't until we got into the problems of survival that we really began to think of water as a necessity for life. In survival situations in the bush, you have two choices: you either go down in a spot where there is water available, or you carry your supply with you. The issue, then, is how much did we need?

We have already discussed the physiological need for water to keep our bodies functioning, which requires three pints a day per person. If we break this down to terms of "glasses of water", it is *six* eight ounce glasses of water daily—or the equivalent. Not all of the "water" has to be aqua pura; you may ingest it as soup, milk, coffee or in meat and vegetables which have a great deal of water content. We will get to the discussion of food in a moment, but the point here is that five gallons of water will supply all the liquid two adults will need for about a week. A couple of quart canteens will suffice only for a day or two, which is about the basic minimum for most downed airmen to cope with. As we will get to later, "reconstitutable" foods cannot be reconstituted without water, and they are the heart of our survival kit preparation. When planning to make a long cross country flight over any but heavily inhabited areas, we include four gallon jugs, in addition to the four quart-capacity canteens of our survival kits. That way, we won't be caught short if they can't start looking for us for a few days, say, because of weather.

Meeting the Second Requirement: Shelter

The importance of shelter for survival cannot be over-emphasized, for more people have died from exposure after survivable landings in the wilderness than have actually been killed by impact. It is vitally important to keep warm, dry and, more than that, as comfortable as possible.

Staying in the Airplane

If the airplane's fuselage is in a level attitude and you can be sure that there is no danger of fire from leaking fuel, there is no reason for not staying in the cabin, although it has been my own experience that even with the seats removed, it is hard to be able to stretch out in comfort in most lightplanes because of spar locations and recesses for passengers' feet. In spite of those minor discomforts, as long as the plane's windows and windshield are intact, the cabin will offer some waterproof and windproof shelter until something else can be rigged.

Keeping Comfortable

It may strike some people as droll to speak about keeping comfortable after going down in the outback, but it is possible if one is both mentally prepared and physically equipped to do so. All it takes is a bit of advance planning. Let's begin by talking about clothing requirements.

Foul Weather Gear

Most foul weather gear made of rubberized or other impermeable types of material will surely keep one's clothing from becoming
sodden by rain, sleet or snow, which is important because most cloth
when wet loses its heat-retaining or insulating qualities. Unfortunately, slicker-type rain coats and trousers create another hazard:
because they are impermeable, any heat generated in the wearer's
body is retained, as in any rubber suit, so that the clothing worn
under it becomes sodden from perspiration, with the same effect on
its loss of insulating qualities, since it totally blocks any evaporation.
It is recommended that you do not engage in any exertions or labor
while wearing rubberized rain suits, especially in extremely cold
weather.

Because of this, we carry our military ponchos (nylon waterproof covers about eight feet square with a drawstring-closable head
hole at the center) which will keep us dry in a downpour without the
steam room effect, since ponchos so worn are open along the sides.
Furthermore, with reinforced holes (grommets) at the four corners
and spaced along the edges, ponchos can be rigged to form temporary emergency shelters in the woods merely by driving a few nails
into convenient trees and stringing some nylon cord to form a
windbreak or a pup tent.

Lean-to Construction

A jury-rigged tarp or poncho is strictly a short term proposition,
usually for the first night, when you haven't yet gotten yourself
organized. However, if you have time (i.e.: daylight) enough a better
shelter can be fashioned merely by cutting a few saplings about an
inch in diameter (assuming you are reasonably near a stand of trees)
and creating a framework on which a tarp or poncho can be draped or
stretched to create a windbreak, as well as shelter from rain and
dew. A properly constructed lean-to (usually with a 45° pitch) can be
heated into the comfort zone by a reflector-type open faced fire by
the radiant heat, even when there is a slight breeze, if the ends of the
structure are closed off. The shelter should be long enough for one
or two people to stretch out at full length parallel to the source of
heat, to get the full effect of the radiation. Sleeping with either one's
head or feet closest to the fire can quickly become uncomfortable. Of
course, any time an open wood fire is involved, great care must be
taken not to have one's clothing, sleeping equipment or shelter (or
the surrounding area and its trees) inadvertently ignited by flying
sparks.

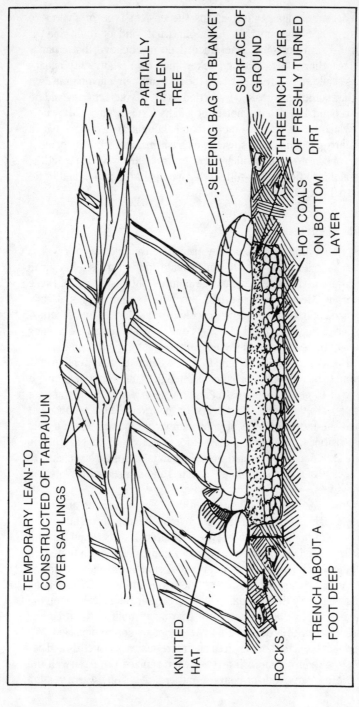

TEMPORARY LEAN-TO
CONSTRUCTED OF TARPAULIN
OVER SAPLINGS

PARTIALLY
FALLEN
TREE

SLEEPING BAG OR BLANKET

SURFACE OF
GROUND

THREE INCH LAYER
OF FRESHLY TURNED
DIRT

HOT COALS
ON BOTTOM
LAYER

KNITTED
HAT

ROCKS

TRENCH ABOUT A
FOOT DEEP

Coals from camp fire, covered by three-inch layer of dirt in a shallow trench can provide warm undersurface for sleeping bag. Fallen tree is utilized for lean-to construction.

The simple lean-to is perhaps the easiest type of shelter to fashion, but brings up that question: what kind of tools does it require? From personal experience, I do not believe that a hand-knife, whether it be a folding pocket knife or a heavy duty sheath knife is really adequate to perform the task, although given time I am sure that something could be whittled to fit. My selection would be either a hand axe or a machette, or a light "cruiser" axe. My wife's idea (which has a lot more merit than I thought at first) is a pair of heavy duty garden or tree shears which will make quick work of most bushes and limbs up to an inch thick. It also helps to have a length of twine along to tie the cut-to-length saplings into position and to tie the tarp/poncho to them.

Natural Shelters

In most mountainous or hilly areas one can find caves, caverns and rocky overhangs which can provide immediate shelter from precipitation. However, it must be pointed out that many of these quarters in Mother Nature's Hotel may have other clients already ensconced and who may resist forcefully any effort to evict them— or to join them. In natural hideaways one may find animal life ranging from bats to bears, so don't ever count on just moving in and taking over. Besides, most caves tend to be too damp for an extended stay and tend to be not only cool but dank enough to mildew your shoes. It is difficult to get a good, restful night's sleep if you think you hear displaced wolves, foxes, wildcats or bears padding around just beyond the flickering light of your campfire, just waiting to assert their positions. Something else: the objective in all search and rescue situations is to remain as conspicuous as possible and alert to the passage of aircraft overhead, which is another reason for keeping out of caves.

Other natural shelters frequently appear in wooded areas, for example partially fallen trees which may be readily used as the ridgepole for building a lean-to type of shelter. If the ground beneath the fallen tree is not perfectly suitable, you can dig out a bed-sized area below it and turn the dirt over while removing stones, roots and underbrush to create a spongy sleeping surface. Experienced woodsmen carry this sometimes a step further, especially when the ground is cold. They will start a roaring campfire, then dig the bed-sized area to a depth of maybe a foot or so, reminiscent of a shallow slit trench, then begin to fill the trench with hot coals and hot ashes to a depth of an inch or two, then replace the dirt (with the rocks, etc., removed, of course) and create a soft, warm resting

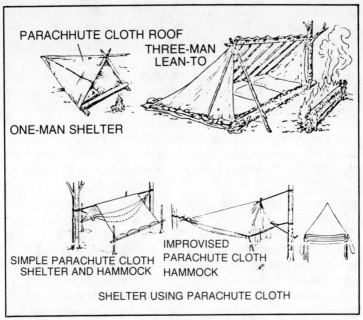

PARACHHUTE CLOTH ROOF

THREE-MAN LEAN-TO

ONE-MAN SHELTER

SIMPLE PARACHUTE CLOTH SHELTER AND HAMMOCK

IMPROVISED PARACHUTE CLOTH HAMMOCK

SHELTER USING PARACHUTE CLOTH

While the Air Force is big on parachute shelters, the private pilot can employ same ideas using plastic sheets packed in survival kit.

place. A major tenet of woodsmen/outdoorsmen is never to sleep on the cold, hard ground and this is one of the easiest ways to avoid it.

About Tents

We have noticed that there is a tendency to dwell more on how to make snares with shoelaces that to discuss toting tents in airplanes, but it is a fact of life that a downed airman may be exposed to severe weather for at least part of the bivouac and must be prepared to cope with it; there is no other choice.

Since the issue is survival, there is no need to carry a large cabin-type tent. All that is required is some form of basic protection from the elements, rain, snow, sleet, wind—and small creatures of the woods, including gnats and mosquitoes. Two-person tents vary around the ten pound top limit, usually lighter if made from treated nylon, which we recommend. So, it is not too heavy for the emergency kit that may save your life. In wintertime, particularly.

Anyone who heads for the woods or mountains with the intention of communing with nature will usually carry some kind of shelter along. It may be on wheels (a camper, a van) but most real woods loafers use tents. For extremely cold weather survival situations, a

61

good tent in the survival package might spell the difference. There is no better way to cope with exposure to severe weather and in winter one must be prepared to cope with it for at least a part of the stay in the wilderness.

Since the issue is survival, not pleasure camping, there is no need to carry a large cabin-type tent. All that is required is some form of basic protection from the elements, rain, snow, sleet, wind and perhaps small animals. A two-person tent which weighs about ten pounds and has its own aluminum formers to hold it in shape, made of treated nylon is recommended for anyone who is going to fly wherever there is a chance of heavy snow accumulation or frigid air and high winds.

Keep in mind, when looking over the array of tents in the sporting goods store or trail outfitter's that whatever you buy will not look quite as nice when erected as the ones set up indoors. You must take into consideration that the tent will have to be set up in inclement, possibly violent weather, windy, cold and wet, so it can pay to have a tent that will go up with no complications, such as rigging support lines to tent pegs and fly-roofs. A wide variety of lightweight models, sometimes called "mountain climbers tents" or "backpackers tents" are on the market, many with their own built-in aluminum support battens. It is well worth taking a look at them.

Tube Tents

Because so many commercially-available survival kits feature "tube tents", a term that is new to most of us, a word is due them, in passing.

Most of us think of tents in terms of size and capacity with the compact, one or two-person "pup-tent" at the bottom of the list, moving up through the slightly larger "A frame", then the pyramid styles, some of which can have floor areas with 24 feet on a side, 576 square feet—about size of a pretty good living room—certainly larger than the living space on any boat less than 80 feet long. Of this group, the tube tent is closest in size to the pup tent and is a product of recent technology.

Tube tents are literally tubes made of a continuous sheet of polyethylene and about eight feet long. The thickness of the plastic material can be recognized by the fact that an entire tube tent can be (and comes) packed in a container about the size of a can of beans, so that many tube tents seem to be about the thickness of medium weight or *light* weight trash bags. We recommend that you ascertain what the thickness of the polyethylene or polyeurathane covering is, before trusting your survival to one. Our ground-cloth emergency

The space blanket. This useful item has aluminized layer of material that reflects back 80% of your body heat for warmth. In hot weather it reflects away heat. It's windproof, waterproof, washable, and flexible to 60 deg F below. With corner grommets to build a wind break, sun shade, or survival tent, it measures 84 in × 56 in. Courtesy Eddie Bauer, Inc.

polyeurathane "tarps" are *three* mils thick; medium weight trash bags are *two* mils and light weight trash bags are *one* mil thick, to give you some basis of comparison.

Better-quality tube tents come with reinforced attachment holes (grommets) to which lines must be attached for both support and holding both its shape and position. If there are no trees around, and/or no supporting lines, the tube tent is worthless. We carry our own light nylon cord and recommend that you do so, too. We do not recall any emergency kits featuring tube tents that have included support or anchoring ropes.

The good points about tube tents is that they are very light in weight and very inexpensive and very compact. However, as any-one who has loaded a trash bag knows, they can easily be punctured and will rip and tear with hardly any stress. Our conclusion is that they are strictly short-term emergency shelter and are protective only in dry, calm weather. Try for yourself: cut the end out of a trash bag and make a jockey-sized tube tent and rig it in your back yard or on the roof of your apartment house, or some place where the wind can get at it, and see what happens to that open-at-both-ends tube. Then, imagine trying to get a restful night's sleep in it.

As said before, we prefer to have a heavy (3 mil) plastic "tarp" with grommeted edges as our first-line emergency shelter, plus a poncho for each of us. A 9′ × 12′ plastic tarp can also be used as a groundsheet which is very important for sleeping on the cold, damp ground, for it provides moistureproof insulation beneath your sleeping bag, even when it is raining outside your tent or shelter.

Survival Clothing

Although few of us consider that garments worn on one's body is a form of shelter from the elements, that nevertheless is exactly what they are, with possible exceptions of, say, bikinis. If you have ever stepped outside on a cold winter night without a coat or gloves, you recognize the truth of this. Having appropriate clothing to surmount a survival situation is necessary just as much as having fire-making equipment.

Hot Weather Clothing

Clothing requirements for surviving in a warm or hot climate are simpler than those required for an extended stay in, say, Minnesota in February or in Alaska, but the basic need for shelter is still there, plus protection from excessive sunburn and from insect life.

Sunburn is regarded by most people as being either therapeutic or cosmetic and everyone looks better after proper exposure to Old Sol. But the key word is "proper." Excessive exposure to the Sun's ultra violet rays can cause a serious physical problem, possibly death.

It gets back to the medical fact that the skin is an important organ in our metabolic system. If exposed to the glare of the sun, so that it becomes "burned" (and a severe sunburn is about the same as a gasoline flash-fire burn) the surface of the skin so affected loses its ability, because of the damage incurred, to produce perspiration which is nature's normal way of cooling the body through evaporation. This, plus the fact that the kidneys will be affected by poisons circulated by the blood can lead to all kinds of physiological problems, including chills and fever, nausea, diarrhea, severe headaches and a

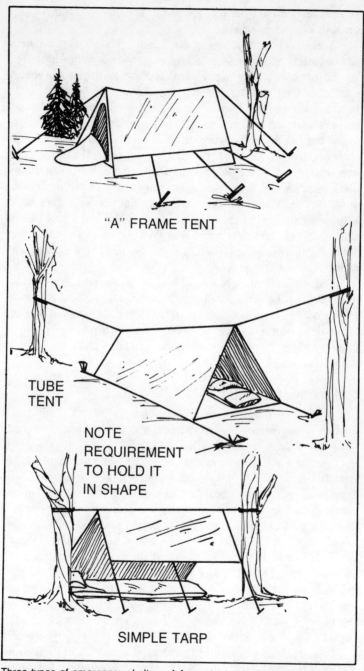

"A" FRAME TENT

TUBE TENT

NOTE REQUIREMENT TO HOLD IT IN SHAPE

SIMPLE TARP

Three types of emergency shelters: A-frame tent, tube tent, and simple tarp windbreak.

loss of skin through peeling. All this in addition to the fact that a sunburn is in itself painful.

This situation must be guarded against. You should have long-sleeved shirts, long trousers, gloves and a wide brimmed hat unless you already have a heavy tan. Even that doesn't always mean you are safe. One time we were on our way home from a week in the Bahamas where I had been doing a lot of bonefishing while dressed only in shorts and a sun hat, so that I picked up another layer of tan on top of the one I had from my vacation several months before. By chance, I dropped in at an Out Island airport just as the diving group was heading out, so we joined them. Dressed only in bathing trunks, mask, snorkel and fins, I spent the brightest part of the day face down on the clear water, my back constantly awash. Five hours later, we returned to the dock and that night I had a real case of sunburn shock, complete with the shakes and upset stomach which put me into bed for a couple of days. So don't fool around with sunburn in semi-tropical or tropical regions.

Aside from that, it is a good idea to have insect repellent and mosquito netting in your hot weather survival kit. I carry a mos-quitoproof head net to wear over my hat when sleeping out of doors in mosquito country. Once, while on a camping trip I could not open my eyes in the morning because mosquito bites had my eyelids as puffed as a couple of marshmallows.

Cold Weather Clothing

When the temperature drops below 40°F/10°C, one faces another very serious hazard, particularly if there is any breeze. Unless well protected by insulating material, a human body which operates at a normal temperature of 98.6°F will radiate off a lot of heat, whereupon the first symptoms of hypothermia appear: To keep itself warm, the body activates muscles to warm them up, causing what laymen call "shivering", a form of which is teeth-chattering. After that, the body's protective mechanisms take over; blood supply to the extremities is reduced or cut off in order to conserve the body's core heat so that the viscera will continue to function. Sometimes the blood supply cut-off to fingers and toes becomes so extreme that they become gangrenous—dead and de-composing. It is difficult to reverse this physiological trend and get the blood flowing outwards again. There is a lot of wisdom in the Alaskan adage that "It is easier to *stay* warm than it is to *get* warm".

The cold air situation is worsened if the air is in motion, no matter how slight the breeze. Air moving across any heat-radiating surface literally pulls the heat out at a predictable rate which is greater than the heat loss if the air is still. This is known as "chill factor."

As an illustration: If your face is exposed to 40°F air which is in a mild, 10 mph breeze, the effective or equivalent temperature on your unprotected skin in 30°F—below freezing! If the free air temperature is 15°F, a ten mph wind drives the equivalent temperature down to 0°F (or − 18°C) well within the frostbite range. And if the wind picks up to 30 mph, the equivalent temperature dives to − 25°F (− 33°C), where exposed flesh can freeze within 60 seconds! For this, you must be prepared. You cannot survive, unless you do. This is why we carry waffle and fishnet underwear, wool socks, thermal boots, wool shirts, pants and jackets and goose down filled jackets, hats, trousers and face masks in our Cherokee Six when heading out to the cold country.

From the Skin Out

In the event you have never heard of it, I would like to introduce you to a recent development known as "fish-net" underwear. It is made into a peek-a-boo mesh which looks like, well, a fishing net, but worn under wool clothing in winter, its openings or "interstices" seems to operate somewhat as a skin diver's wet suit: by trapping pockets of warm air in the openings, it keeps the body warm, yet at the same time allows perspiration to pass, so that it does not become damp. If worn under woolen clothing, perspiration can evaporate right through the cloth.

Wool is an almost unique fabric because it has the property of retaining its heat-retaining or insulating qualities even when it has been immersed in water, as in falling through the ice of a lake, and it will eventually dry—although it will be mighty dank and uncomfortable. But it also has the amazing property to pass moisture— perspiration—through, thus allowing the skin to breathe. The combination of fishnet—or wool "waffle" knit, which is about as good— underwear, with outer layers of woolen clothing makes a tremendous combination. Friends who live and work in cold climates advise that, rather than wearing one heavy wool coat and pair of trousers, the best way to dress for cold weather where one will be engaging in physical exercise, such as hiking, logging, hunting or chopping wood for the fireplace, is to wear several light layers of woolen clothes, so that body heat is built up the outer layers can be peeled off like the skin of an onion. When the heavy work is over, the layers can be gradually replaced so the body can cool itself without becoming chilled.

Most of the time our woolen clothing, including several extra pairs of socks, glove liners, scarves and watch caps are carried in a survival bag. We always take extra socks and gloves so that we can change them every day and be able to wear a pair that is dry and hopefully clean, if we can wash them. If water is in short supply it is enough to air-dry damp wool socks, shirts and underwear. If you do have water, you can hang woolen clothing out and let it freeze solid, then beat the ice off with a stick and let the few crystals that remain disappear by sublimation—the direct transformation of ice to vapor—leaving the clothes completely soft and dry.

There is absolutely nothing that will surpass high quality goose down-filled garments for warding off the cold. I began using down-filled jackets years ago on early spring fishing trips and now have a wardrobe that will handle conditions all the way to forty-below. Normally, when setting off on a business trip, where I am wearing "city" clothes for a mid-winter meeting, I put on an Eddie Bauer quilted parka and quick-removable quilted long pants, to keep—as the saying goes—warm as toast during the interminable cold weather procedure of the pre-flight check, including loading the cold-soaked airplane, untying the frozen tie-down ropes and getting the engine started and warmed up. Once aloft, when the cabin heater takes over and warms the plane up, I can unzip a couple of zippers and whisk the pants and parka off without getting out of my seat. I don't know how we ever got along without quilted clothing, and Eddie Bauer's are unsurpassed.

It is extremely important that you keep your clothing clean and especially that you keep it dry at all times. If your clothes ever become wet, you must dry them immediately; never wear wet clothing, even wool clothing. One of my good friends went through the ice of a lake last winter when crossing aboard a snowmobile, somehow extracted himself from the icy water, crawled to dry ground where he gathered a huge pile of brush with the aid of a heavy-duty pocket knife and started a huge bonfire (he always carries matches in a waterproof container, a plumbers candle, a knife, a whistle and a compass when out of doors). Then he removed all of his clothing and stood naked while the fire dried his sodden garments and incidentally kept him warm as long as he kept turning around. He came out of the experience without so much as a case of the sniffles. It shows what one can do if he doesn't lose his wits.

Normally we can all anticipate that socks and glove or mitten linings will become damp from hand and foot perspiration in the course of a day, no matter how cold it is. They can be dried easily by exposure to the fire, or else by taking them to bed with you all night,

A piece of cold weather survival gear that may be considered is the Optimus catalytic handwarmer which delivers up to 10 hours of flameless heat, weighs but two ounces, and fits in a pocket. Courtesy Eddie Bauer, Inc.

which will take some of the dampness out. If it really gets cold, there is an old Alaska bush pilot's trick that works: turn the mitt linings and socks inside out and leave them outside. Then in the morning, beat the ice out of them with a stick.

Comfort at Night

We have already alluded to the fact that it is almost impossible to keep operating at top efficiency without adequate rest. Therefore time spent in considering how to achieve this important objective is well spent, indeed.

Woolen clothing, down-filled parkas, thermal boots, face masks and headgear that encloses the whole head and neck will keep the effects of the extreme cold off during the hours you are up and about, but another problem arises when evening falls and it is time to get some sleep. Again, this is a time to be as comfortable as possible, because if one is to continue to be alert, strongly active and *healthy*, it is necessary to regain strength by sleeping restfully and soundly every night, while waiting to be found and rescued. It all adds up to a need for comfort.

The rule of thumb is that warm, protective sleeping equipment is required any time the overnight temperature drops below 70°F/ 21°C, especially if any kind of a breeze is blowing. Sleeping under inadequate protection can lead to muscle chill which leads to painful stiffness and possibly to partial incapacitation. It can also lead to pulmonary diseases, colds—with chills and fever—and to pneumonia. At the very least, when the weather is mild, a couple of woolen blankets are needed. In any event, the best bet for survival in the wilderness is to assemble an ample supply of warm clothing, sleeping bags, ground covers, inflatable (or foam rubber) mattresses and rain protection—and take it with you. Don't ever count on being able to make it by living off the land.

Despite all the pretty artistic drawings and photographs in survival books, a bed of pine boughs doesn't hold a candle to a down-filled sleeping bag on a foam rubber pad. Once, as a candidate for a Boy Scout of America award called the "Wood Badge," I made—and slept on—pine bough beds under pine bough lean-tos and always wound up with back pains, head colds and smelling of pine sap, with pine needles in my hair.

In addition to sleeping bags, many outdoor suppliers, including Sears Roebuck (and don't scoff at *their* top o' the line equipment!), can fit you out with compact, lightweight two and four-person tents, many of which contain their own built-in supports for simple and quick setting up without the need for tent pegs and guy ropes. These windproof structures are far superior to anything constructed of branches and bushes, even those built by an experienced out-doorsman. Especially when the outside air is below freezing and a breeze is blowing, snuggling down in a sleeping bag inside a small tent is preferable to a shelter of sweet-smelling pine boughs.

Sleeping Bags

It is unlikely, probably impossible for anyone to get a comforta-ble, restful night's sleep if his body becomes chilled, if for no other reason than that the temperature-regulating mechanism of the human body will quickly set up both warning signals and follow them with a pattern of involuntary muscular activities to create heat in

Parka and trouser combos filled with goose down are ultra-warm and ultra-light; outer fabric is windproof and water repellent. Protection to −40 degrees F. Courtesy Eddie Bauer, Inc.

those fibers in which the operating temperatures has been reduced by exposure to the cold.

The early warning signal is a wake-up signal, a pattern of restlessness and vague bodily stirrings and sensations of awakening occasioned by discomfort, possibly by triggering a shiver-reaction. Since at least a quarter of your time will be spent sleeping—normally one-third is, but nervous energy will cut that down somewhat—it is essential that you have a sleeping bag that will meet the requirements for survival under the worst of conditions you might encounter. It must also be kept in mind that your metabolism will be affected by your physical condition, or lack of it. If you are out of shape to start with (and, let's face it, most of us are!) and physically tired and hungry, you may want to have a sleeping bag that will offer extra protection from the chilling wind of the northern tier. It is vitally important that you be able to keep warm, no matter how cold it gets.

Sleeping bags come in two basic forms: the rectangular, or bedshaped, and the "mummy", which is, well, shaped like a mummy. For intentional camping out, we prefer the rectangular type, particularly the types of which two individual sleeping bags can be zipped together to make one large two-person bag, which is cozier in many ways. However, mummy bags are lighter in weight, provide less dead air space and are easier to handle and pack. And ours can also be zipped together into one bag.

Without getting into all of the niceties of sleeping bag design and fabrication we recommend that you examine the labels on any sleeping bags to ascertain that the bag is not the "sewn-through" or the "box sewn" types, both of which will frequently develop cold spots inside the bag. Much more desirable are *differential* cuts where the seams of the inner and outer layers are arranged to prevent the inner and outer seams from coming together and allowing cold air to seep in. As for filler material, there is nothing that will beat good goosedown for warmth, either in clothing or sleeping paraphernalia. Its main, perhaps sole disadvantage is that when it becomes wet, it loses most of its insulating quality and it is very difficult to dry out. For this reason, many outdoorsmen are using bags filled with some of the new, synthetic fibers which are non-absorbent and will dry quickly, even if immersed.

In any event, read the label on any bag that catches your eye and determine what that bag's "comfort rating" is, that is: the temperature range that the bag is designed for. Although it is really only an approximation, it will steer you away from the summer-type bags right from the beginning. What we have are down-filled bags rated "from 50°F to −10°F (−23°C)," just to give you an example. They weigh less than 8 pounds.

A Last Word About Sleeping Bags

Remember that you perspire while sleeping, even in the wintertime. Furthermore, if it is really cold, we all tend to sleep with our heads within the warmth of the bag (anyone who has done any cold weather camping will confirm that moving one's face to a cold spot in the pillow, as in turning over, will wake up even a sound sleeper out of doors) so that the interior of the bag will become humidified. As a result the bag will become damp. Then during the day, it will become clammy and dank. Hence, every sleeping bag must be turned inside out and aired at least every other day, whether the climate is hot or cold. If it is really cold, the accumulated dampness will quickly show up as light frost soon after the bag is opened up, but it will disappear by sublimation in a couple of hours and will be dry. Of course, it will

Skyline sleeping bag is available in three comfort ranges, regular length, large, and long. Filled with goose down, this model may be zipped together to make a twin size. Courtesy Eddie Bauer, Inc.

be cold, though, so if you don't want to crawl into a cold interior you will have to pre-heat it with warm stones from near the fire. or by holding it before the fire for a few moments before retiring.

...And About Mattresses

Camping manuals to the contrary, sleeping on the ground is uncomfortable, particularly for anyone who has not been trained, or learned the hard way, how to do it. No matter what, to assure a good night's sleep, we recommend an air mattress or a foam rubber sleeping bag pad which can be laid out on the place you are going to wear your sleeping bag. Our experience is that, in cold weather, a "closed-cell" foam pad is better insulation, but any kind is far superior to simply throwing your bedding on the ground cloth and climbing in.

...And About Bed Clothing

Plan to sleep in wool clothing. However, always try to have *dry* clothing to wear to bed—at least next to your skin—and wear dry woolen socks to bed (or some other kind of foot warmers; we use Eddie Bauer down-filled booties). And a warm head covering. And put your water supply where it won't freeze, like near the campfire.

Which brings us to the subject of how to make a campfire in the first place.

Meeting the
Third Requirement: Fire

If you have water and shelter, the odds are pretty good that you will survive for a day or two. But fire is of equal importance for lengthly endurance. The relative importance of water, shelter and fire may be likened to the requirement for three sound legs on a milking stool: if you take away any one of them, the other two will not support it. You must also have a fire.

The Basic Need For Fire

Most people think of campfires in terms of burning logs with forked sticks erected on either side to support another stick festooned with pots and kettles of hot coffee and hot food. Modern technology has given us better ways to prepare food than over an open fire, but it must be said that there is more to a good fire than cooking. The crackling and flickering brightness of a wood fire has a mesmerizing effect on all of us and creates a feeling of warmth and well-being, even when only in a living room fireplace.

When it comes to spending time out of doors, having a fire becomes much more important, because it is sort of an atavistic security blanket. At night, particularly if one is not used to it, things can get pretty spooky in the dead of night. Animals move about, wails, screeches and bumps will be heard, especially when dead tree limbs fall to the ground with a resounding crash, and it is not unusual for a city-type person to imagine that, out there in the darkness a bear is stalking its dinner: him. Being out in the open where one can see the stars and the moon is of some help, if the skies are clear. But life in the wilderness is so far different from what most people are used to that a large, roaring fire is needed, if for no other reason that as a psychological crutch. Which is reason enough.

Laying a Fire in the Woods

Before you can have a fire in the woods, you must prepare it. First, you must clear an area of combustibles such as pine needles, leaves, dead branches and roots. It is bad enough to be on the ground after a forced landing without being in the middle of a forest fire that you have started yourself.

Then you must prepare tinder, kindling and fuel for the fire and have a good supply of all three. Tinder—easily ignited material to start the fire going—can be made by using a sharp knife on a dead limb to form curlicues of wood (a "fuzz stick") or a pile of well-dried leaves, pine needles and small sticks. Kindling is the next size larger dry limbs and branches from dead trees. Once these are brought up to the ignition point by the flames from the tinder, they will flare up and ignite the larger pieces of fuel and make the campfire. In real life, pieces of crumpled newspaper, which most of us seem to have kicking around somewhere in our planes, is far superior to pine needles and fuzz-sticks. Or, if you have no newspaper, you can use pages from your deceased airplane's operating manual and collection of Airworthiness Directives.

All of this is pretty elementary, of course. What is important is that, while it may be difficult to prepare, or "lay" a fire and to light it—which we will get to in a moment—the hardest part is *keeping it going*. It requires a lot of wood, more than you can break from dead trees with your bare hands. You will need tools.

Fire-Laying Tools

Few tools surpass a well sharpened machette for cutting dead limbs from trees or chopping down small trees up to four inches in diameter, whether alive or dead, including ridgepole pines that are featured in so many idyllic camping scenes. It is a great instrument for assembling a pile of burnable wood and we always have one in our plane. But the size of the wood it produces really falls into the kindling category. To gather a supply of those larger six and eight inch in diameter logs featured in survival and camping manuals, all so neat and even-sized, you need more than a sheath knife or a machette. To cut down sizable trees, even dead trees, then to cut them into usable lengths, requires an axe. I recommend what is

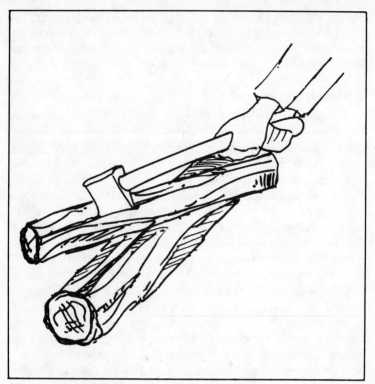

The proper way to split a log for the fire.

called a "cruising axe" which, with a head weighing less than two pounds and a 24″ handle is larger than a hatchet or hand-axe, yet not too large for the average person to use or to carry. We include one in our large survival kit.

Recently, while on a flying trip to Canada on a fishing foray, I saw, in the luggage compartment of a Canadian bush pilot's plane a small, gasoline powered chain saw which struck me as a great idea. Boy, would that make the job of collecting wood and clearing an area easy! Some outdoors writers believe that a handsaw is superior to an axe, and I think that they have a good argument, especially in the case of anyone who has not been trained in the use of an axe. Even a folding crosscut saw will produce even-length logs for the fire as fast or faster than an axe in untrained hands and with less danger to the wood cutter. And, as reported earlier, my wife has just about convinced me that a pair of heavy duty long handled garden shears will do a better, faster, more exact and safer job of assembling kindling and cutting down small saplings than even my well-used machette.

A Few Words About Edged Tools

There are three phases to survival equipment, including sharp edged tools: (1) you have to have it to use it; (2) you have to know how to use it, and (3) you must take care of it. In the case of axes, perhaps more than any other tool you must add that you must be able to use it *safely*. An axe can be a very dangerous instrument. It can kill you, or injure you so badly that you cannot survive. Be warned!

To be worth anything any edged tool must be sharp. I mean *sharp*. The old gag shot of northwest woodsmen shaving with the blade of a heavy double-bitted axe is no gag. I have seen axemen hone axe blades until they were literally razor sharp. When an axe is that sharp there are only two ways to be sure that it will not slice you accidentally—and remember now, I am talking about a single-edge or single-bit axe: You must keep it in a sheath when it is not being used, or you can bury its sharp edge in a piece of tree trunk if it is dry, dead wood, otherwise it will rust. When carrying a sharp axe, keep the edge turned away from your body. I saw an axe catch on a tree limb which twisted it just enough to scoop the right front pocket off a logger's jeans. By all means, take your axe out and practice with it, both felling trees and chopping them into useful lengths for the fire and splitting them, which makes them burn better.

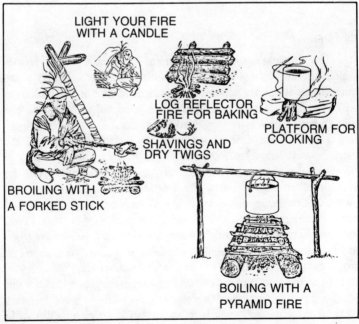

Types of camp fires.

The normal routine is to clear away all of the lower limbs and underbrush around the tree so that there will be nothing to interfere with or deflect the arc of your swing. Don't swing hard. If the axe blade is sharp, it will kick out good sized chunks of wood even though you feel as if you are taking practice swings. To direct the fall of a straight tree, you can cut notches on each side of the tree, alternating the sides from which you swing and keeping the lowest cut low, no more than a foot or 18 inches from the ground. The big hazards are standing too far from the tree, or too close to it so that you do not get a smooth motion. And the real hazard of a dull axe is that it may not cut at all, but glance off and do you an injury. Be careful splitting wood for the fire. Prop it in a cutting-log and take it in easy strokes. Be careful. An axe can be your greatest tool, but it can bite you, too.

Much the same advice applies to knives, too. To be effective as a tool *any* knife must be sharp. For many years I carried a knife in a belt sheath (and still do when in the field) but there are now so many folding blade knives that will do the same job and are less obtrusive that I tend to use them more frequently. The belt knife should be worn off or behind the hip, positioned so that a fall will not drive the blade into your body. Each evening, or whenever you have the chance, hone the edge of the knife (or axe) across a sharpening stone and strap it on the sole of your shoe or on a leather belt. It can pay off.

Camp Fires

The simplest fire is made by ringing a cleared area with stones which will support cooking utensils over the flames. It may be as small as a foot or so in diameter, or as large as four or five feet. This is, of course, really a cooking fire, designed not to burn with too much heat when a low, even heat is required.

There are several classic types of camp fires, including the "star," where lengths of log extending from the point of the fire can be shoved in closer and closer until they are consumed. And the so-called "teepee" fire, in which the fuel is stacked in an almost vertical position, so that it looks like an Indian tent. Most survival and camping manuals include drawings or photos of cunningly constructed baking or heat-reflecting fires. However, we plan not to do any food preparation over open, wood-burning fires. We plan to use simpler, more modern means to prepare our meals.

For the basic confidence-building fire, we believe that the old tried and true log cabin fire (which is the way it looks when we start it) is as good as any, easy to start and to keep going. All that is needed is a good supply of wood and a watchful eye.

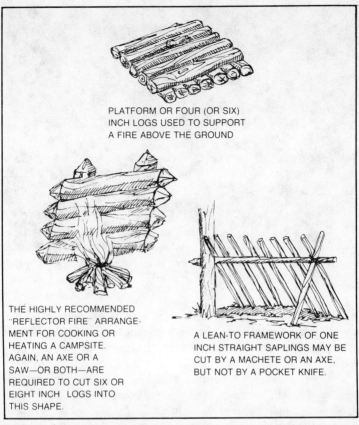

PLATFORM OR FOUR (OR SIX) INCH LOGS USED TO SUPPORT A FIRE ABOVE THE GROUND

THE HIGHLY RECOMMENDED "REFLECTOR FIRE" ARRANGEMENT FOR COOKING OR HEATING A CAMPSITE. AGAIN, AN AXE OR A SAW—OR BOTH—ARE REQUIRED TO CUT SIX OR EIGHT INCH LOGS INTO THIS SHAPE.

A LEAN-TO FRAMEWORK OF ONE INCH STRAIGHT SAPLINGS MAY BE CUT BY A MACHETE OR AN AXE, BUT NOT BY A POCKET KNIFE.

Typical illustrations from survival manuals. No one seems to indicate that none of these can be built with the equipment in any basic survival kit. All of them require an axe or saw.

Fire Starting

Indian scouts, advanced Boy Scouts, survival school trainees from Outward Bound and assorted show-offs can make fire from flint and steel, or by whirling sticks on pieces of dry wood, but I can't. I have tried it, using charred cloth for tinder and all, but damn if I would want to depend on it in a rain and windswept forest. I prefer a sure thing, beginning with the classic, ubiquitous, strike-anywhere, wooden kitchen match. If properly prepared by water proofing there is nothing to compare with it for most fire starting.

Kitchen Match Preparation

Wooden kitchen matches can be waterproofed simply by immersing them in melted paraffin wax, then letting them cool and dry.

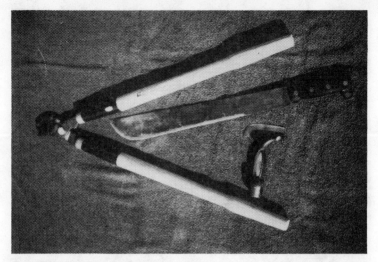

Three items carried in author's emergency kit for cutting brush for kindling and small trees for lean-to construction. The scatchet at the bottom is strictly a' back-up.

We prepare them in several ways well ahead of time, putting them in a variety of different sized packages so that they can be carried in pockets, emergency kits, first aid kits, suitcases and camera bags. We carry a *lot* of matches.

After swishing individual matches through the melted paraffin—which, when melted, has the consistency almost of water—we bundle up three dozen in a little group about the size of a salt cellar, wrap aluminum foil around it and dip the whole kaboodle into the paraffin, one end at a time. Those matches are water-proofed!

We also cut lengths of corrugated cardboard from shipping boxes, and stick matches into the corrugations, something like shoving shells into a cartridge belt. Then we dip them into hot paraffin and wrap the waterproofed "stick" of matches in heavy duty aluminum foil. At the campsite, the cardboard strip can be tacked to a tree so that one match at a time can be pulled out and struck.

We also each carry on our person a waterproof match-safe which has a compass built into its screw-off top. And if there is room in our duffle, I frequently throw in a couple of old pill bottles full of matches.

In addition, we usually have at least one full box of kitchen matches completely treated by pouring melted paraffin into the contents, so that they won't jostle and ignite. Then we dip the entire box in a waterproof sheathing of paraffin.

Three compact, portable cutting tools that meet the need to cut small trees, clean out undergrowth and prepare kindling. The machette has an 18-in blade. Next is a light hand axe. The scatchet may be used as is or a piece of wood can be screwed into it to fashion an emergency light axe.

This all might sound like a lot of trouble, but it beats the hell out of flint and steel or rubbing two sticks together.

Fire Starting Back-Ups

All pilots are aware of the trend to technological redundancy: if one gadget will do the job, but may fail, have another one ready to take over. That is what this section is all about.

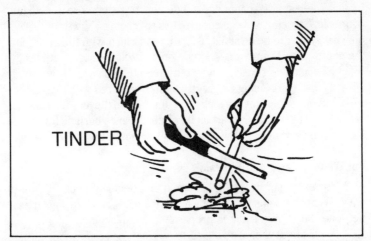

TINDER

Fire making: Striking sparks with the back of a penknife blade on a permanent match.

On sunny days a magnifying glass can be used to start fires *if* proper tinder is available and *if* the fire site can be protected from strong or gusty winds. Starting a real fire by focusing the sun's rays requires some tinder, as a flint and steel does, and we usually carry a little tin box (actually, an old Band Aid can) into which my wife placed some pieces of linen cut from some of my old shirts, then placed the can in the oven at high heat to char the linen slightly and remove all traces of moisture, then (you guessed it) dunked the can into hot paraffin to seal it hermetically. If needed, it will be ready. As an added feature, the can was wrapped with some tissue paper from a gift box, then aluminum foil wrapped around the whole thing. I am reasonably sure that we can start a daylight fire with that, if needed.

Keep Your Tinder Dry

It must be pointed out that the very fineness of the structure of tinder, combined with its excessive dryness so carefully produced makes it especially susceptible to dampness, which it picks up the way a blotter soaks up ink. Hence tinder will quickly become damp when exposed to any moisture in the air, which can adversely affect its fire starting capabilities. Therefore it is important to keep your tinder supply in an airtight container, such as a well stoppered bottle or tin box.

Flint and Steel, Etc.

Although I have never been able to start a fire with real flint and steel, there are indeed those who can and not a survival course goes by that some smarty-pants doesn't demonstrate it before a room full of people. The closest I can come to it is to create a shower of sparks on what seems to be an artificial flint by striking it with the back (not the sharp edge!) of my pocketknife on a gasoline impregnated rag. Maybe I could even do it outside, but I tend to think not. However, I am a big man when using a cigarette lighter, matches with a candle or a magnifying glass. Not too long ago I unscrewed the lens from an old camera and used that to start a pile of dead leaves burning for some kids in the neighborhood. For about ten minutes I was their hero.

But When it Rains and Blows...

However, survival situations may not develop on clear, sunny days. What about starting a fire when it is raining and blowing? It can be done, but again, it takes preparation and planning.

First, about wet wood. We know that "green" wood, either from growing trees or recently cut down trees that were growing,

Plain old-fashioned wooden kitchen matches are about as good for fire-starting as anything. Author carries two large boxes of them, suitably waterproofed by wax treatment. For ease of using, pieces of corrougated cardboard are employed as holders.

resist any attempts at ignition. If you don't believe this, ask someone who has fought a forest fire. The leaves—and pine needles—will burn; the carpet of dead leaves and pine needles will burn; the fallen trees and dead branches lying on the ground will burn—but most of the time the strong, growing trees will survive, even though charred on the outside. If the heat created by the fire rises enough, of course the trees will burn, no matter how healthy they are—and steel will melt and twist and rocks will explode. But short of that kind of heat, green wood won't burn worth a twit. You must depend on dead, that is to say dry, seasoned wood, the kind you can snap in your hands.

Dry dead wood exposed to heavy rain does not become "wet" in the sense of non-burnable. Only the surface will be dampened, at most only 1/8th or 1/4 of an inch in and the water will be eliminated by the exposure to high heat which will dry the wood and it will burn. To prepare kindling from rain-drenched dead wood, you must collect a sizable supply, then split the larger pieces to expose the dry wood within, which can be "fuzzed". If tinder and kindling have been well prepared and protected from further wetting and if the ignition site can be effectively shielded from the wind, you can get a fire started, but it will require a constant supply of fuel to keep it going and, if it is raining, a roof over it of some sort, such as a tarpaulin.

One of the most effective emergency fire starters when a wind is blowing and it is raining is made of fine steel wool and a flashlight battery. To make fire, pull the steel wool out into a length that will form a connection between the bottom and the top (electrode) of the flashlight battery—the steel wool will be a fluffy mass about two inches in diameter and six or eight inches long.

Within a few seconds of closing the electrical circuit, the steel wool will begin to heat up like an overloaded fuse. It will glow, then turn white and, if you blow on it, will ignite like a thermite bomb. The flare-up doesn't last very long—perhaps a few seconds—but you can be sure that it will start a fire if the tinder and kindling have been properly prepared and protected from wind and weather. Since there is only one fire in every clump of steel wool, we carry several of them stuffed into nooks and crannies of our survival kits.

Try this yourself some day. Parenthetically, an even more impressive demonstration can be made if you soak the steel wool in a bucket of water first, then take it out, shake it to remove the water and then run the experiment. But do it out of doors, with a garden hose or bucket of water handy. As an afterthought, we recommend that you consider wearing asbestos gloves.

And Then, There's...

Some other dodges that we don't know how to catalogue: (1) carry a plumber's candle in your pocket and put one in each survival kit. A plumber's candle will burn for a long time and can be used to start a fire in cases where the flame of a match does not last long enough. (2) If the wind is gusty, or even puffy, so that ordinary matches and/or plumber's candles blow out, it is great to have a fire-lighter that will not blow out. We use those trick, self-relighting birthday candles, obtainable in many novelty shops. If three of those are placed together in a tinder pile, at least one will keep burning at all times. Hellova fire starter. (3) In addition to all of the above, we usually carry a couple of cricket-type lighters, guaranteed to give hundreds—if not thousands—of lights.

Back to Cooking Fires

It does not take many experiences to learn that a large cooking fire has certain disadvantages, such as overheating, smoke production and a requirement for full-time attention. Besides, for the most part our menu is planned around dehydrated or freeze dried foods, reconstituted by dropping the contents of packaged containers into a pot of boiling water. For this kind of food preparation, we carry with us a couple of Sterno single burner folding stoves each of which folds down into a small 6-1/2" × 6-1/2" × 3/4" package, but will open into a 4-1/2" high stove with its own wind-deflectors. In it, one can set a can of Sterno "canned heat" cooking fuel which will always light and will boil a saucepan of water about as fast as you can do it on the stove in your modern kitchen. All you have to do is dump in a package of prepared food: soup, hot chocolate, vegetable stew, bouillon or what have you, and you are in business. What we are saying is: you don't have to go through all that fire building routine, just to get a cup of cocoa.

The Sterno stove folds into a flat pack 6¼ inches square and less than an inch thick. Two cans of instant-burning Sterno are packed in the Grab Bag with the stove.

Other Types of Stoves

Many survival and camping texts discuss making cooking stoves from various sized tin cans, ranging in size from coffee cans to one-gallon No. 10 cans and larger five-gallon cans. Over the years, we have built and used such stoves, but do not see any real advantage over the rust-proof, collapsible Sterno stove mentioned above. However, we do have a back-up fuel source, in case we run out of Sterno (which is a jellied alcohol). What we do is cut a strip of corrugated cardboard about 1-3/4" wide and 18" long and roll it up so that it will fit into a catfood can (or a tunafish can, for they are both the same size). Then we slide a piece of cord into the center as a wick and pour melted paraffin into the can until it is filled. Once ignited, the cardboard becomes a wick and produces a reasonably hot fire which will burn for an hour and a half. If the paraffin wax becomes exhausted, it can be replenished simply by dropping a fresh chunk of wax on the top of the can while it is still burning, which will melt the wax and re-form the candle, or burner. In this way, it can be re-used indefinitely. It also can be used in the Sterno stove.

This cat-food-can fire can be used to boil water if placed in a prepared coffee-can-stove and will boil water and fry bacon and eggs on the similar stove made from a No. 10 (gallon-sized) can. But the collapsible Sterno stove is our choice because it is easier to pack and does as good a job.

Signalling Fires

For signalling to would-be rescuers, what is wanted is as much smoke as possible, preferably black, so that no one might think that it is a natural fire, which generally tends to give off a whitish smoke. There are two ways to prepare for this kind of signalling.

The collapsible, easily carried Sterno stove, all set up and ready to cook meat, boil water for reconstituting food, or to make hot soup, tea, coffee or chocolate.

The first way is to drain all the oil that you can possibly eke from the crankcase of the airplane and to collect the tires, inner tubes and anything else that will burn (and for which you have no use) and keep it all in a place near enough to the campfire that it can be dumped on the fire within a minute or two. However, this will not only create a dense black smoke: the odor will put a wrinkle in your skull and once that rubber and oil start to burn, you aren't going to put it out, at least easily. You must have your mind firmly fixed on the thought that *the first aircraft to spot you will not be able to land and take you out.* The airmen will confirm that it is you and will try to fix the spot (even by dropping a fresh emergency locator beacon). But the normal situation is that the first plane overhead will circle a couple of times and fly away, leaving you for another day or two in the wilderness. You should have another fire laid and ready to go for that second search and rescue mission's assistance.

We recommend that a real smoke generating signal fire be built a little way from your campsite, if possible, piled with as much brush and ignitable "trash" wood as you can find—dead pine trees really burn—and be ready to set it off whenever an airplane heaves into view, or hearing.

As a practical matter, once you realize how difficult it is to keep a modest sized campfire going all day and all night, you will understand why it is not possible to keep a signalling fire—let alone more than one—going all the time. Therefore, you will have to prepare a fire that will ignite at the touch of a match or a flare-up from a hunk of steel wool and will burn fiercely within a few minutes and send out a column of smoke. You will have to lay it early in your rescue preparations and protect it from rain or snow. This is where an extra ground cloth or "tarp" comes in handy. A dense black smoke plume

Two types of camp stoves for the wilderness. On the left is a home-made cooker produced from a No. 10 can, cut to accept a heat source and ventillated at the top. At its left is a container of "heat tablets" which will always produce instant heat. Part way into the opening is a home-made burner. The collapsible Sterno stove is at the right.

can be seen from a considerable distance, if the wind is not blowing too hard. If you want the fire to emit white smoke, throw leaves, grasses and pine needles on it, but the oil and rubber smoke really comes out inky black. And a column of smoke can be seen a long way in calm air.

The No. 10 can stove and the three steps in making its candle for cooking: Into a well-washed cat-food can (far left) place a coil or rolled corrougated cardboard cut to size (center). Then pour heated, liquid parrafin wax on the cardboard until the can is filled. It helps to place a cloth wick at the center of the coil. This easily-lighted candle will burn for a couple of hours, and its fuel may be replenished merely by dropping a chunk of wax on the burning area. The author has cooked many meals on such tin can stoves.

Colored Smoke

Combustion-generated smoke is good, but in the last decade sometthing has come along that is better: chemically-generated smoke in bright un-natural colors, both red and orange. There is no mistaking the fact that orange or red smoke is a call for help, even though the person who sees it is not a trained searcher. We will get into this in more detail in Chapter 12.

Meeting the
Fourth Requirement: Food

Let's start off by discussing the nutritional requirements of adult human beings. Food is not, no matter what you may have believed or how much you may have suffered the pangs of hunger while on a weight-loss diet, an immediate requirement for survival. Especially if you are (as most of us) somewhat overweight to start with, you can live for a long time on the energy stored in your body fat—so long as you consume three pints or so of water every day. Although anyone engaging in hard physical labor, such as a logger or steel worker, will consume more energy—more calories—than someone who spends all day behind a desk (or the wheel of an automobile) the rule of thumb is that the average human requirement is about 3,000 calories a day to maintain his (or her) body weight. Since it takes approximately 3,500 additional calories to gain a pound —or conversely 3,500 calories less to lose a pound—it can be seen that a person who is overweight by 15 or 20 pounds can have a slight edge in a survival situation. That is what I keep telling my wife, anyhow. She doesn't buy it.

Food Required

Medical studies of metabolic changes by the armed services have determined that merely by consuming 500 calories in food value a day a person can continue to function almost normally for a great length of time, a month or so, while awaiting rescue. He may be hungry most of the time, even dream about food, but except under exceptionally cold conditions, which require additional calories, he can operate, as long as he has an ample supply of drinking water.

Food Availability

As we have said many times this far, it is possible to stay alive—to survive—in the wilderness without food, as long as we have water, shelter and fire, but if we are to survive *comfortably,* you must stoke the old boiler. Having been through a time without food (a week) after which my only food was coconuts, Vienna Sausages and Fruit Cocktails (for eleven weeks!) I certainly don't want to go through hunger pangs and starvation-shock again, nor do I want to have the same menu day after day.

Berries, Roots, Seeds

Classic survival books dwell heavily on edible fruits, roots, berries and living creatures of various forms that may be available to provide nourishment, with such advice as:

> All grass seeds are edible....

> There is generally more nutritional
> value in roots and tubers than in
> greens....

But, they caution:

> Do *not* eat mushrooms unless you are
> an expert in identifying edible from
> poisonous species....

> Do *not* eat plants that exude sap that is yellow/
> orange/red/dark/soapy looking
> or milky, except papaya, wild figs and
> dandelions....

> Do *not* eat the nuts and seeds of fruits ....

But, about the time they get to recommending a permissible menu of such morsels as snakes, lizards, insect larvae and grubs, tree bark, properly prepared (?!), seaweed, worms and grasshoppers, I tend to close the book.

Local Food Availability

There are many places on the North American Continent where one can live off the land, especially if he is properly equipped and trained to do so. Survival would probably be easiest for even a minimally equipped person in a seashore environment, particularly if he were able to land on a broad, hardpacked beach and the nights were not too cold. Ocean beaches offer more in a survival situation, both for food gathering and successful discovery by air-searchers, than almost anywhere else an airplane might go down. I have always felt comfortable whenever a beachline is in sight, whether it be the Atlantic, which we fly along regularly between Boston and the Florida Keys, or the rim of the Gulf of Mexico or of the Sea of Cortez—or beaches on islands in the Bahamas or the Caribbean. I know that along those strands I can find birds and animals and usually fresh water a short distance inland. Seafood abounds in most un-fished waters and it is astonishing how much firewood (properly "driftwood") accumlates on remote beaches.

At low tide all kinds of shellfish, including clams and mussels are there for the plucking, or digging, and they can be eaten raw, or cooked. Using a piece of heavy gauge aluminum foil spread over hot coals from the wood fire, clams in their shells can be laid out in rows; as soon as they open their shells they can be taken off the "grate" and eaten, well-roasted. Close in to the beach, fish can be taken with a net, a fish trap or with a hook and line, which is part of one's survival equipment, and is the easiest way to put fish on the menu. At night the larder really becomes ambulatory: when darkness falls most beaches literally crawl with crabs foraging for food in the surfline. Both crabs and lobsters can be caught on handlines baited with inedible (to humans) parts of deceased fish; all one has to do is tie a fish head or other parts to a line, toss it into the ocean just beyond the frothing surf and wait for a while, maybe ten minutes. Then, by hauling in s-l-o-w-l-y on the line, the crab or lobster which is enjoying its dinner so much that it refuses to let go, becomes one's next meal. Both lobsters and crabs can be prepared for eating merely by dropping them alive into a pot large enough to contain them whole. They can be boiled in either salt water or fresh water, although fresh water is recommended. Usually fresh water can be obtained by digging a hole inland several hundred feet from the beach, since rainwater seeping into the ground, being lighter (less dense) than the sea water which permeates the seaside area tends to float above it (a process known as natural stratification), lies in a layer somewhat above sea level. That is how wells dug into the porous oolitic lime-stone of the Bahama Islands work. However, as a passing note, if by accident a well-pipe is set so deeply that it pierces the dividing line between the salt water and the freshwater, called the "interface", the entire supply can homogenize and ruin the drinkability or potabil-ity of the entire water supply. But a well or water hole dug only a few feet down can usually produce at least a seepage that can be col-lected in a vessel such as a canteen cup or a pot—or a shaped piece of aluminum foil. In a pinch, all fish and crustaceans can be eaten raw *if* there is a good supply of drinking water to keep the kidney system flushed.

There is another time-honored method of cooking all forms of sea food, especially crab mussels and oysters but also applicable to fish that have been cleaned.

This technique requires only a shallow trench dug in the soft sand to a depth of perhaps eight or ten inches and building a well stoked fire in the depression, using whatever combustables that are available in the vicinity. When a good layer of hot ashes has been formed, next step is to place a layer of wet seaweed previously collected from the beachline, covering the fire, then lay whatever is to be cooked on the seaweed layer, first wrapping it in a protective layer of some sort, then covered with another layer of seaweed. For New England clambakes, canvas is usually used as a wrapping, although sometimes the food is cooked in pots placed in the pit. But as good as any wrapping—perhaps better—is easily handled aluminum foil, which is one of the greatest survival tools one can have. Sometimes, where there is a lot of clay in the ground, it can be molded to the food to be cooked.

In addition to fish and shellfish, the seaside provides other types of food. Sea birds: gulls, terns, sometimes ducks and geese and pelicans, fly over and land on beaches or on the water just off the beach and can be easily taken with a survival gun if it becomes necessary.

As one proceeds southward towards warmer waters the surfside menu increases. Turtles may be found at night on many beaches and inhabiting inland fresh water ponds and streams. Turtles provide excellent sustenance, besides which they cannot run away and hide. If you catch one, all you have to do is turn it on its back to immobilize it while you obtain the means of dispatching it for the pot. It pays to be careful, for a turtle's beak can take a chunk out of you easily and quickly.

A fresh water snapping turtle may be harvested by annoying it with a stick at which it will not only snap but lock onto tenaciously so that it can be raised from the water. A quick stroke from a sharp knife to sever the head is the first step to preparing it as food. I have seen turtle heads cling to sticks for hours, so you must be very careful when handling them. Large sea turtles, found in the warm waters of the tropics and semi-tropics offer a great amount of nutrition and a sizeable population of green turtles can be found in the Bahamas, the waters of the Caribbean and parts of the Gulf of Mexico. Since they are practically without natural enemies once they have grown beyond a certain size and have developed an impregnable carapace, sea turtles sometimes grow as long as six or seven feet from stem to stern. However, most of the turtles found in the areas we have flown are in the three to four foot range, or smaller, and are presumably more tender to eat. They can be caught ashore, turned over and disposed of with almost any kind of weapon, from a club to a large rock.

All turtles can provide both meat (turtle steaks are a delicacy in gourmet restaurants) or a fine soup (ditto) and produce both high protein and high caloric food (406 calories per pound, approximately). Preparation of any turtle is essentially similar and relatively simple. After cutting off the head, run a sharp knife blade along the skin where it joins the shell, pull the skin off the feet about the way you pull off a pair of socks, then disjoint the legs at the "knees." Then remove the lower (or under-) shell by slicing through the connective tissues. Remove the entrails (the technique of cleaning game will be discussed in detail a little later on). This will expose four pieces of meat still attached to the top shell, which should be removed with the sharp knife.

Cut into no larger than inch-sized cubes, the meat can be dropped into boiling water which should then be left to simmer for ten minutes or so after which the meat can be removed and eaten and the remaining broth can be poured off and consumed as well. Turtle meat can sometimes be a little on the tough side if the critter is old and large, but most of the time it is succulent, tender and rich, and made more so by broiling or baking, using the bed of coal and aluminum foil wrapping technique described above. Gourmet cooks can do all sorts of things with turtle meat by using an assortment of wines, spices and sauces: snapper soup, green turtle soup, turtle steak, all are featured in the best restaurants. But even without all of the goodies of modern culinary art turtle meat can be quite palatable. Some of the tastiest turtle meat I ever had was prepared by a kid in the Turks and Caicos Islands who baked it in a five gallon can buried in hot coals. The following day he did a chicken for me in the same way, with the same can.

Other Treats From the Sea

One of our sons, a highly trained food and beverage man in the hotel business, was recently based on a Caribbean island. On a visit, he produced for a cocktail, time snack a dish that looked like and moreover tasted like some variety of fish eggs, mostly reminiscent of golden salmon roe. It turned out that he had taken the afternoon off, donned a mask, snorkel and fins and dived off the hotel's dock to collect a bushel basket of those poisonous, prickly-spined pincushions known as sea urchins. Wearing heavy leather gloves for protection—anyone who has ever accidently stepped or backed into a sea urchin knows how painful a spine embedded in the skin can be!—be broke off the spines, turned the creatures on their backs and opened them up with the point of his sharp knife to expose the little clumps of roe which he then carefully dug out to go with our rum swizzles. Of course only the female urchins produce the delicacy and I never have learned to tell which is which until they are opened up.

He also introduced me to another source of food which is considered as top fare by natives of the islands but which I had never considered: sea cucumbers. Having observed them over the years crawling across the bottom of shallow seas, sometimes marooned as the tide went out and left them helpless, it had been my reaction that although when at rest or depicted in a photograph or drawing they might look like its garden-grown namesake, in real life the crawly sea-thing presents a certain aspect of oozy obscenity. My son explained (after I had unsuspectingly eaten the unusual tasting morsels) that he had prepared the sea cucumbers (gulp!) by peeling off the skin and taking out the four lengthwise muscles thereby exposed. He also told me that they could be eaten raw. (Double gulp!)

And of course, there is always something relaxing about fishing either from the surf or from a pond or from a stream, which is why we always have a fishing rod in our Cherokee Six.

Other Natural Foods

However, nature's provender is by no means restricted to beaches fronting on the ocean. Food is everywhere.

It comes as a surprise to city born-and-bred people that even in a gaunt and dreary desert there is an abundance of living things which survive although the annual rainfall may be less than what the more verdant areas of the north and east receive in a couple of weeks. This is the land of the black-tailed jackrabbit and the food chain that supports it—and that it supports. The wild game situation is appreciably better in the other areas, which have enough water to supply copious plant life, for that usually means that both animals and birds will be in evidence. And, of course, if you are near a stream, pond or lake there is a strong possibility of adding fresh water fish to your diet. It pays, therefore, to be prepared to harvest the food crop that nature has provided.

Fresh Fish

Being an inveterate fisherman, I always have a fishing rod and an assortment of lures, lines, leaders and other accouterments of a devout nimrod, stored in some nook of our cars or airplane. Usually they are encased in those protective aluminum tubes with which fishermen are familiar, from three to four feet, four inches long. The cases are required to prevent breakage of the fragile sporting rods, some of which, while six or eight feet long, when assembled, weigh in at a scant two and 1/2 ounces. However, fishing for food when you need it, as in a survival situation, is not necessarily a sporting proposition and any way you can put brainfood on the broiler is fair, whether it be by baited hook, gill nets, a fish gig or a hand grenade.

However, when we began to play the game of let's-make-up-your-own-survival-kit, we began to look around for a fishing rod that would fit in an 18″ long carryall bag, similar to the largest commercial survival kit we had seen. That, of course meant that we had to find a fishing rod that would take down to fit the bag.

There are a number of "packers' models," take-down rods that can be disjointed to make a more easily carried package. One example, the one I got myself for Christmas, is an Eddie Bauer "Micro-Mini Pack Rod" which is made of fiberglass, measures five feet long when assembled, takes down into 11 separate sections, none of which is more than six inches long, weigh 2-1/4 ounces and comes in a pocket-sized case. The reel, etc., of course are extra. It is a great rod with surprisingly good action, despite all the ferrule-joints.

A year or so ago, my wife gave me another fishing rod for the airplane survival kit, and I must confess that when I opened the package, I thought it was a child's toy. It wasn't. It was one of the most useful and practical fishing rods in my extensive array.

It is called "The St. Croix Fishing Machine"—sort of a corny name, which led to my erroneous conclusion—and consists of a five foot long fiberglass spinning rod that telescopes to 15-1/4 inches and contains its own built-in spinning reel with eight-pound test nylon monofilament normally supplied. Of course other weights of line can be substituted, but the eight-pound line seems excellent for a survival tool. I have used my Fishing Machine to catch bass, lake trout, brook trout and bonefish and look upon it as a great addition to my fishing gear, whether for sport or for survival. And you can always find one in our airplane, with a plastic box containing lures, hooks, swivels, split shot and a pair of needle nose pliers taped to it.

We also carry in our survival kits small containers which include a 300 foot length of monofilament line, several plastic floating "bobbers", a number of drop-lines to which hooks can be attached and strung from the bobbers, and of course, a supply of new, sharp hooks. Festooned with worms or grubs, and left afloat on the surface of a lake all night, there is a reasonable assurance that there will be fried fish filets on the breakfast bill of fare. Not sporting, maybe. But nourishing.

Fresh Meat

There is always the possibility that one might have to survive entirely on provender supplied by nature, not necessarily including manna. What we are talking about is small (or perhaps, large) game indiginous to the area of your temporary adobe. The advantage of having wild game on the menu is that it provides animal fat for the production of caloric energy, approximately twice as much as is produced by the ingestion of pure protein, so that if it appears that a lengthy sojourn in the wilderness is in the offing efforts should be made to obtain this important caloric requirement from animals and birds.

To give you an idea of how much caloric value there is in wild game, most nutritionists claim that each pound of edible meat in commonly found wildlife of North America will produce the following by roasting:

Muskrat	700	calories	per	pound
Turkey	870	"	"	"
Opossum	1000	"	"	"
Beaver	1100	"	"	"
Raccoon	1150	"	"	"

In the coldest part of winter, when the ground is covered with snow, there is a great amount of wildlife activity both on the surface and in the air over North America's northern tier. Birds are everywhere, including crows, grouse (which comes in several varieties) and the ptarmigan, which is protected in Canada because it is so unafraid that one can approach a bunch of them perched on a tree limb and knock their heads off with a stick. There are rabbits, hares, squirrels, beavers, muskrats and, of course, the waddling porcupine which is so well protected by its quills that it is not afraid of man or beast and—like the ptarmigan—can be approached and taken with a club or a rock wielded by a hungry lost hunter. Or downed airman. Once, when caught out in the bush on a late fall canoe trip which froze over the lakes on their route, two of my friends came across a porcupine as it munched on a clump of berries, knocked it on the coco and then wondered what to do with it, since neither of them had any tools or utensils except their pocket knives, match-safes, hand compasses and candles. Their preparation was pretty rudimentary:

Collapsible fishing rod. The compact telescoping St. Croix "Fishing Machine" is small enough to be carried in any vehicle, including an airplane.

they built a big brush fire, tossed the porky carcass on it, quills and all, and let it cook—innards and all. After most of the quills burned off, they retrieved the somewhat singed remains, skinned it, cleaned it properly and buried it in the hot coals. After a while the well-cooked porky was removed, washed clean of ashes, carved into chunks and eaten, not necessarily with relish. One of the fellows remarked later that, although he wouldn't order it in a restaurant, it sure was good on that cold, lonely night. It is amazing how good anything tastes when one is really hungry.

Game Getting

Assuming that you do not want to have to depend on a wild game menu which depends on walking up on birds or animals that can be brained with a club, the question that must be answered in any survival situation is: How do you procure such wild game? And, how to you prepare it for consumption?

Most survival manuals discuss at length, backed up by some rather idealized artists' drawings or carefully staged photographs (I say this, because I have never been able to duplicate them) how to make snares, traps and dead-falls for the purpose of supplying the food requirement of the downed or isolated person. Maybe those things will work, although I have never been able to make one that would, and I have tried. In addition to the frustrations involved in

97

repeated failures, it seems to me (maybe I am rationalizing) that, as in the case of the solar still, the work involved will expend more caloric energy than even a successful effort will replace—since any small game so acquired will not supply as much as 1200 calories a day, which any Weight-Watcher will tell you is a weight *losing* diet.

For the benefit of the unenlightened, a "snare" is engineered to snatch the animal either by the neck or leg and it will kick and struggle until it strangles to death or is happened upon by a carnivore who takes quick advantage of its helplessness and eats it alive before the trapper returns. The "trap" grabs by a foot and holds the animal a prisoner of pain and with the same result of hours of fear and the real possibility of attack by predators. Although I did not set it, I saw the effect of a "deadfall" one time while on a fishing trip in Georgia. A deer had been lured by a block of salt as bait and had been unable to free itself from the large deadfall that had been placed by a primitive backwoodsman, who undoubtedly needed the meat for his own survival.

Unfortunately, the deadfall had not killed the deer, which I heard thrashing around as I was walking through the woods on my way to a trout stream, so I unlimbered my 35mm camera and went to investigate.

The deer had apparently been there for some time, with its head caught under the fallen tree, for an arc had been cleared of leaves and brush where the helpless animal had scrabbled in its attempts to escape and as I approached it was obvious—there was an electric feeling in the air—that the deer was desperately frightened that it was going to be killed by another animal. When I tried to lift the log, it was too heavy. Then I saw the deer's mouth and knew that releasing it would be of no use: its lower jaw had been broken and torn half off in its struggles and it was going to die of starvation even if turned loose. Sadly I got out my anti-snake pistol, loaded it with a couple of high velocity .38 Spls and shot the deer in the ear, killing it instantly and releasing it from its agony.

What I am getting at is, for obtaining game for my own survival, forget the snares, traps and deadfalls. I would rather make a clean, instant kill with a bullet.

Survival Guns

Few issues are more controversial as this is written than firearms and there is no intention in becoming involved here in that highly charged emotional issue, where reason and the ability to communicate fly out the window. We will limit our discussion to the basic theme of firearms as tools for survival in the wilderness.

A Few Basics

There is no such thing as a "pip-squeak" firearm. *Any* firearm discharged in the wrong direction can cause a wound at least as serious as having a ten-penny nail driven into living tissue, whether it be a wild animal or a human being. Therefore, before relying on *any* kind of firearm for survival or protection purposes you *must* receive at least some basic training in safety and the accurate direction of firing the weapon. Firearms, *mishandled,* are dangerous and can be lethal.

Firearms fall into major classifications: shoulder guns and hand guns, both of which terms are self-defining. Let's talk about shoulder guns.

Shoulder Guns For Survival

First, *rifles.* For the hunter, several dozen cartridges and loading combinations of powder and bullets are available, from the old black powder .45-70 (caliber 45/100th of an inch and loaded with 70 grains weight of black powder) down to the .30-30 and a series of center-fire, superspeed .22 "varmit" rifles. The number of models of .22 rimfire rifles is astonishing: I stopped counting at 27.

But for the emergency or survival hunter the elephant/lion/moose rifle loads are not really required. All that is needed is a small caliber rifle which will produce accuracy with negligible recoil and be able to use ammunition that is light to carry and small enough to store in quantity in the emergency kit. And the rifle itself must also be small enough to fit into an emergency kit, too. After having surveyed the field pretty thoroughly, we settled on the .22 long rifle cartridge and began looking for a suitable rifle.

Ubiquitous and Ample

Three items that can be found on the shelves of stores in almost all parts of the world are (a) Hershey bars, (b) Kodak film and (c) .22 long rifle ammunition. People who don't know one end of a firearm from the other and are bewildered by references to the .30-'06, .243, .30-40, .300 Magnum, .375 Magnum or .450 H&H, recognize the term ".22". Some people who should know better make fun of it and call it a "pip-squeak," which irks me, as I have already said. Let me tell you why: in three different locations on separate occasions, I have observed ranchers slaughtering sizeable animals: pigs, horses and cattle, where the creatures were dispatched with a close-up head shot from a pistol loaded with .22 shorts. One shot was usually all it took. In view of the fact that the .22 long rifle high-power loads are many times more powerful, and yet have no flinch-generating recoil, we went for that.

Ultimately we selected a rifle specifically designed for downed-airman survival, since most of the rifles we tried stretched out to about three feet even when disassembled. For a time, we carried a surplus military .30 M-1 Carbine, which is really a shoulder gun chambered for a high speed pistol cartridge, but it seemed too powerful for small game and not powerful enough for defense against large animals. Our choice, therefore was the AR-7 "Explorer Rifle" made by Charter Arms Co. The AR-7 is an eight shot, semi-automatic .22 long rifle with a 16″ barrel and it takes down without tools, so that the barrel, action and eight shot magazine clip all fit inside the plastic stock for protection while not being used. Furthermore, so stored it is waterproof and it floats. As a matter of fact, it will also float when fully assembled. So, the very first time I saw one, I bought it immediately and after having shot it thousands of times both for target practice and for plinking—for it is a wonderful fun-gun—I have only the highest recommendation for the AR-7. I chose the Explorer Rifle over all other rifles for inclusion in our survival kit.

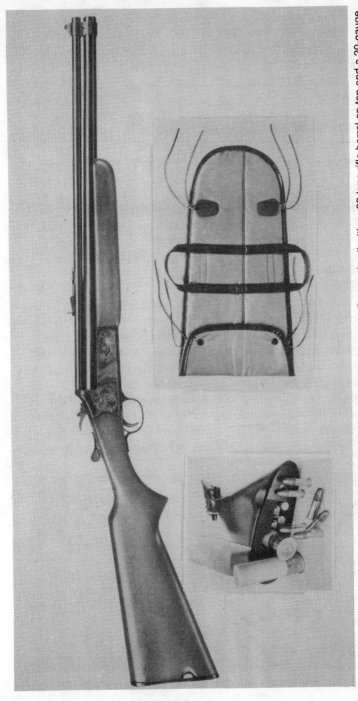

This may be the ultimate survival weapon, the Savage Model 24-C "Camper's Companion," with a .22 long rifle barrel on top and a 20-gauge shotgun barrel below, and selective trigger. The butt provides storage space for spare ammunition.

While on a fishing jaunt to northern Maine, I noticed that our guide had a shoulder gun attached to his pack and after a day or two—you can't rush into these things in Maine, y'know—I asked him what kind of a rifle it was.

"T'aint a rifle", he said, with which he pulled it out of its case and handed it to me for inspection. It was a well-worn compact pump-action 12 gauge shotgun with rifle sights and a carrying sling, the Ithica Model 37 Deerslayer. For some reason, I had not really thought about a shotgun as a survival weapon up to then. He set me straight.

A 12 gauge shotgun is probably the ultimate all-around survival weapon, where weight is not a primary consideration. It weighs about six pounds, empty and a box of 20 shells adds a couple of pounds more. But talk about versatility! Loaded with No. 8 shot, it will take most small game; with No. 6 shot, medium game and with No. "0" buckshot will kill a deer. On top of all that, loading it with high velocity slugs makes the 12 gauge capable of knocking a wild steer off its feet at short range.

While I was thinking it over back home, eyeing the assorted shooting irons in my gun rack, I picked up an outdoor magazine and read an article that really touched an exposed nerve.

It was about a bush pilot in Mexico whose single engine plane had suffered engine failure and had to make a landing on the beach in a totally uninhabited and very isolated area which was seldom traversed by lightplanes. It took the better part of a week for anyone to realize that he was missing and to start a search, so he was theoretically going to be in tough shape when they found him—if they found him, for all he had was a canteen of water...they thought.

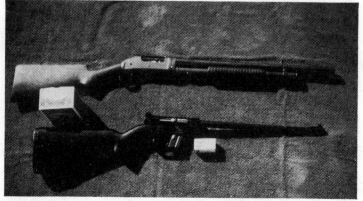

The 12-gauge shotgun and the AR-7 .22 semi-automatic set up for use.

The 12-gauge shotgun at the top has a 20-in barrel and fits easily into the emergency kit, the "Red Bag." The AR-7 .22 long rifle at the bottom (shown with barrel and action stowed inside stock), is lighter than many handguns, and a lot more accurate for most people to use.

When they found him near his wrecked plane, he was fat and sassy. He had ripped off a cowling and bent it to make a container for sand, into which he poured some gasoline to make a fire. He removed the stuffing from a seat frame, leaving only the squiggly metal supports, which he used as a grill to prepare quail, dove, partridge, ducks and a small deer from the area. He had a folding knife, some paper matches—and a 16 gauge shotgun, with a supply of No. 8 shot, which kept him in food.

That did it. I plucked the little-used Winchester Model 1897 pump I had inherited from my father, hied to the local gunsmith and had the barrel cut back to a legal 20″ (which made it cylinder bore), then took it out to the shooting range with a supply of assorted shells. I am convinced that there is not a survival situation that will be beyond my shotgun's ability. The Model '97 goes with us, too.

If this seems to contradict my earlier-mentioned requirement for lightness, it doesn't. The weight problem in a weapon to be *carried* can be critical, for the woodsman's rule of thumb is that you should carry along 100 rounds of ammunition, and I will guarantee that 100 large rifle cartridges are a back-breaking load after a few miles on foot, whereas 100 rounds of .22 ammunition can be carried in two small boxes weighing only six ounces each and can be dropped into a pocket without any burden.

The post-crash survival problem is different, for the best plan, which we shall analyze in detail, is generally to stay in one spot until someone comes to rescue you. Therefore, the shotgun will be kept in the vicinity of the campsite and the weight of the gun and its ammunition is not really a major factor.

Combination Guns

Many years ago, while dove shooting, one of my companions was using a very unusual-looking shotgun of European design known as a "Drilling." He claimed that there were probably not a handful of them in the United States, although once in a while he heard of one in Mexico or Central America, for he was a collector of the rare arms. He lived, as I recall, in New Mexico. The Drilling is a multi-barrel gun, made some time in the early 1900s with two shotgun barrels mounted in the then-conventional side-by-side fashion, with a third barrel below, to form a triangle and a fourth barrel centered in the triangle. The smooth bored barrels were in 12 gauge; the lower rifle was in, as I recall, .30-30 and the fourth barrel was chambered for the .22 long rifle. At the time, it seemed a little much, but now I was looking at guns from a somewhat different perspective. For some time, the Savage Arms Co. has been making two-barrelled "combination guns" that would seem to be almost ideal survival guns: rifle barrels mounted above shotgun barrels in various combinations of caliber and gauge.

At the invitation of a friend who owns a Savage 24-V, I went out and did some informal trap shooting off his back patio (the nearest house is two miles away) and was really impressed. His combination was a .222 Remington on the top and a 12 gauge on the bottom, but I believe that I would prefer the 24-C "Camper's Companion" in .22 long rifle and 20 gauge, which weighs only 5-1/4 pounds and stores in a case measuring 5" × 22" × 3-1/2". Both .22 ammunition and 20 gauge shotshells are lighter than the larger loads and the 20 should supply as many birds as the 12 especially if one waits until the birds are sitting. Remember, just as in the case of fishing, we are not talking about shooting for sport but to ward off starvation. And to do it better than by snares, traps and deadfalls.

Handguns For Survival

Most firearms controversy swirls about handguns, which some people look upon as innately criminal, manufactured "only for the purpose of killing someone." Well, let me make one statement and get on with the survival issue. I have carried a handgun for most of my adult life, almost as regularly as I have worn a tie, and I have never (a) held up a bank, (b) robbed a gas station, (c) murdered anyone, or (d) threatened anyone, although I have records of police officers and former policemen who have—including one who murdered a mayor. My interests in handguns are two: (1) defense of my person and family, and (2) shooting as a form of recreation, either in formal range shooting or plinking. No, better make that three: (3) Survival.

Pistol Pros and Cons

The biggest argument in favor of a pistol is that it is the best back-up weapon to a rifle or shotgun available, far better than a knife, or an axe. Furthermore, you can easily keep it with you, when visiting the latrine, cutting wood, replenishing the fire, dumping garbage, doing any of the little chores where one would not normally sling a rifle or carry a shotgun or have one immediately at hand. I know of too many instances where a pistol has saved someone's day—if not his life—to dismiss handguns lightly. I have had a few experiences where I was mighty glad that I had one along strapped on my person.

One time I was walking alongside a New England trout stream in late summer when I suddenly realized that I had accidentally strayed between a large black sow bear and her cub. My hair stood on end, for a momma bear will attack viciously if she thinks her baby is threatened and there was no way I was going to reason with her, win a foot race with her, or climb a tree while wearing my waders, fishing vest and all the stuff that goes with them. There was no way I could have staved her off with my 2 ounce fly rod or my camera, but tucked into my belt under my waders was a Ruger Single Action .357 Magnum and if that bear had attacked with blood in her eye, I would

Two handguns formerly carried by the author for keeping porcupines, raccoons and snakes out of the camping area. At top is a Colt .22 long rifle single action; at bottom is a .38 Special Colt Cobra. Both guns have been replaced by the AR-7.

105

have used it in self-defense. As it happened she and the cub got together without any problems, as far as I was concerned. But it took about an hour for my heart to get back to normal.

I have already told about the deer caught under the deadfall, which I put out of its misery with the Colt loaded with high-speed .38 Spl. ammo. On the same trip—same day, in fact—I was walking camera in hand with my friend and host (it was a huge private hunting and fishing preserve) looking for some of the elusive feral cattle that had developed as a herd from a few that had swum ashore from a shipwreck many years before. Except that, we were the ones being stalked. A broad-chested longhorn bull with a tip-to-tip span of more than four feet snorted and appeared over a hummock, obviously spring-loaded to charge. I was frozen to the spot, armed only with a Nikon, but my friend had his Ruger .44 Magnum in action as the bull lowered his head. And that was that. Again, having a handgun saved us from possible harm.

For many years I carried the .357 Magnum in its holster in our grab-bag, really as a defense weapon, though we had the AR-7 .22 in the plane. However, it was a case of being over-gunned for most situations, so we replaced it with a smaller Single Action, a .22 with two cylinders, one chambered for the .22 long rifle (same as the AR-7) and the other chambered for the .22 Rimfire Magnum which is in itself a pretty powerful loading for close-in self defense. We also have a good supply of .22 RM shot cartridges for taking small game and birds close-in, but also excellent anti-snake protection in heavily infested areas.

The Cons...

It does not take long for anyone to learn that a pistol is at best to be considered mostly as a long knife, a last line of self-defense against a dangerous opponent. Unless highly trained and with a background of constant practice, it is almost impossible for the average person to keep bullets on a target the size of a bread box from a distance of 75 feet. Therefore it should not be counted on by anyone who does not have the background to supply the table or pot. As for bird-getting, I am not sure, but I would not want to depend on it.

Furthermore, because of the anti-handgun bias of many people and laws against having them in so many States and localities—as well as in Mexico, Canada and the Bahamas—we have given up carrying any handguns with us in the airplane. But we still like to shoot them for fun.

The Morale Factor

A while back, we talked about the psychological need for a fire when isolated in the wilderness. The same thing is true about firearms, *if* one is properly trained in their use. It has to do with the mental attitude or confidence to endure a situation and to prevail, which is known as "morale." Having a firearm that one knows how to use for protection against wild animals makes an immeasurable contribution to one's feeling of security, even though it is never used. As long as I have my well-oiled Model '97 stoked with "0" buck and a couple of rifled slugs, it is difficult for me to visualize any situation I couldn't cope with.

This is in itself an important yet frequently overlooked consideration in contemplating a stay in the wilderness. No one who has never spent any time out of doors in the woods, or on the plains—or for that matter a night on the beach at the seashore— can have any concept at the bustle of activity that begins as darkness settles over the area. A region that has produced only the twittering of a few birds and the chattering of squirrels capering in the trees can become, as night comes on and changes the setting, a veritable cacophony as nocturnal breeds emerge to hunt for food and fight for their lives. The first exposure to the noises of nature can be a truly terrifying experience for a big city type whose only contact with nature in the raw has been by making a financial contribution to the Friends of Animals. And it must be added that when it gets dark far from the electric light glow of civilization, it really gets dark! So dark that perhaps for the first time in one's life all of the visible stars in the sky, from one horizon to another, stand out brightly and details of the surroundings can be seen by what used to be considered the faint light of the full moon. It can be scary to the camper on his first time out, but far worse for someone who has just undergone the trauma of experiencing a forced landing and busting his airplane. Under those circumstances it is easy for fear to become uncontrolled and blossom into panic which takes away one's ability to reason. The fundamental atavistic animal reaction to flee a situation which is considered personally dangerous and with which one can not cope—the frightened animal syndrome—can result in one's bolting to escape, leaving the accident site and thrashing headlong into the brush. This can lead to terrible consequences. Many air searches have successfully located downed aircraft reasonably intact, only to have the rescue party find it empty since the occupant (or occupants) had panicked and run off. The number of instances where their bodies have been found months later by hunters or hikers is shocking. But it gets back to the morale factor. There is no denying that merely having a firearm in his (or her) possession and knowing how to use it so that one has the ability to defend against any kind of attack creates a self-assurance, or confidence that inhibits the build-up of fear to the point where it becomes panic. This is an aspect that should never be discounted when it comes to planning whether or not to include a gun of any kind in one's survival kit. Just having it may save your life, even though the firearm never actually has to be discharged.

Advice About Hunting

If you have any background or experience in hunting in wooded or rugged country, what I am going to say may be elementary—and it is. But if you have not had it, read carefully.

The first and most important rule about hunting is *don't get lost!* This applies whether you are hunting for big game in the Canadian Rockies, the African veldt, the mountains of Maine or just walking around with someone else's survival book in hand, looking for edible berries. No experience is more nerve wracking than becoming disoriented when on foot and being unable to relocate the position of the base camp you have left, whether it is a hunting cabin in the woods, or the wreck of an airplane. It is so easy to get lost that no one believes it until it happens, so you must plan ahead not to.

There is a common misapprehension that the personal magnetic compass included in survival equipment is there so that the downed airman can navigate back to civilization on foot. This is wrong, as we shall discuss later about "walking out." The principal use of the hand-held compass is to navigate in the vicinity of the campsite, as when collecting firewood, going to the latrine, searching for water, or hunting (even if hunting only for berries). It is easy and common for people to become lost the moment they are out of sight of the base camp, whether in heavily wooded territory or in terrain having many mounds and depressions so that one can lose sight of landmarks. I have become lost within 200 feet of a campsite when cutting wood.

Any time you leave the immediate vicinity of the campsite, it is imperative that you carry a magnetic compass, for what you must do in effect is made a dead reckoning out-and-back plot just like you did on your early triangular cross country flights, or the way sailors do, except that you have to do it on foot. If you start off for any reason, take a sighting to a landmark tree and go to it, write the route you have taken (this is why all woodsmen have pencil and paper in their on-person emergency kits) and make a mark or "blaze" on a tree, bush or other object so that you can find your way back on the blazed trail. Some of my friends carry pieces of dayglow paper or Hallmark

A BLAZE MARK MADE BY BREAKING A BRANCH FROM A SMALL TREE TO INDICATE A TURN TO THE RIGHT

A TRAIL BLAZE MADE BY PILING UP THREE STONES

A BLAZE MARK ON A TREE MADE BY CUTTING OFF TWO SQUARES OF BARK TO SHOW A TURN TO THE RIGHT

Types of marks for blazing trails.

yarn called "Gift Tye" and thumbtacks to blaze their trails and one uses clumps of yellow ribbon to show the way back to camp.

In addition, you should always have a good, high quality police whistle on your person whenever afield away from camp. I would never rely on the cheap plastic whistles I have found in the commercial survival kits since I know that my life may depend on my whistle producing a loud, clear note, no matter what kind of a beating it make take in handling. Everyone on board should have a police whistle for signalling his or her position and I recommend that the whistle be hung (along with a magnifying glass) around one's neck on a cord, so it won't get lost. The piercing and characteristic sound of a police whistle will carry appreciably further than a shout and never can be confused with a sound of nature. By making three quick blasts in succession, which is the universally recognized emergency signal in the woods, one can obtain immediate attention from anyone within hearing range. Even someone with a broken rib condition, which makes shouting impossible, can blow a whistle hard enough to be heard for a hundred yards. Which raises another problem meriting discussion and another warning: *Don't get hurt!*

It is important to recognize that proceeding on foot in the woods or in the rough, especially those crisscrossed with rocky hills and fast flowing streams, is dangerous! A turned ankle, a sprained knee, a broken bone or a serious cut incurred while engaging in any physical activity such as jumping across a stream, or stumbling over a tree root, or falling off a ledge or chopping wood, can immobilize you far from the safety and protection of the base camp, including fire and food. When in any kind of wilderness, take your time and make every motion as carefully and cautiously as a coyote approaching a baited trap, for that is what nature in the rough is: a baited trap, waiting to catch the unwary. Don't move unless you can see clearly where you are going to step next. Snakes are not the only problem, even in the copperhead-ridden Poconos; turning—or worse snapping—an ankle in a chuckhole camouflaged by fallen leaves can have fatal results.

What this all adds up to is that most hunting in rugged territory will be restricted to the hours of daylight when you can see where you are going—and stepping. Remember, in dense woods sunlight comes late and disappears early in the day. An old meat-hunters trick (quite illegal but extremely effective) is to shine the brilliant beam of a six cell flashlight at deer in the darkness of night, engaging in what is known as "jacklighting" deer. For some reason the animal becomes mesmerized by the light and stands perfectly still as long as it shines, producing an easy killing shot. It may work for an accomplished woodsman who is out to feed his family, not for the sport, but my advice is never to try it, no matter how hungry you may be, if it means leaving your camp when it is black out there beyond the range of the firelight. If you want to learn what it is like, get invited on a Tennessee or West Virginia coon hunt and see what night hunting is like. At least there will be a bunch of other nuts out there to help you get home.

It's Not That Easy

Hunting wild game is not as easy as the anti-hunters of the Bird and Bunny Protective Association seem to think when they say that the game doesn't have a chance. Wildlife, that is *wild* life in the wilderness, not in the vicinity of built-up communities, is extremely wary. After all, predators survive by catching other animals and eating them alive, so it must be obvious that the hunted creatures which fall into the classification of small game (i.e.: edible) tend to melt away into holes, dens, nests and natural cover whenever they feel threatened, which is of course the way they survive in the first place. Even though they may not have had any personal contact with and are therefore not afraid of "man," they are sure as hell afraid of other life-forms and a human being moving in their vicinity will trigger their instinct to hide. So, don't expect to sit by the fire and pot food for the pot, even if you have a shotgun. It may take some forays afield. And you won't succeed with every shot.

Some Basic Hints

First off, if you do buy a firearm of any sort, make arrangements with someone to learn how to use it safely. You must know how to load it and to unload it, how to disassemble it for cleaning, how to carry it so neither you or your companions can possibly be injured by an accidental discharge. It helps if you consider (1) that *all* guns are loaded all the time and (2) that they can go off at any moment, for at least you will keep the muzzle pointed in a safe direction. You should be able to hit an object the size of a tennis ball, consistently, at 300 feet, otherwise you will be wasting irreplaceable ammunition for your rifle. A shotgun's range is more likely to be 100 to 125 feet, no more.

When hunting, you must move through the woods or brush as quietly as possible, stepping carefully so as to avoid snapping dead branches underfoot; a half-inch limb snapping sounds like a pistol shot in the woods and you can count on not seeing anything move for several minutes. If you go thrashing through the woods like a two legged bulldozer, or slashing a trail with a machette, or smoking a cigarette or pipe, you can forget hunting, for the senses of wild animals are phenomenal. They can see, hear and smell far beyond the normal ranges of humans and any untoward movement, sound or scent will send them scurrying for cover until the warning of possible danger has passed. So a hunter must move slowly with stealth, stopping frequently to listen to the sounds of the wilderness. For the first few minutes, when the game has been alerted, it will be quiet. Then little sounds will start up: birds chirping, squirrels chattering and the tentative, cautious movements of all kinds of animals that had "frozen" at the first sign of danger. Sometimes it can take as long as 15 minutes of the hunter's motionless posture before the wildlife community slips back into gear. If the hunter makes another noise there will be a new pattern of bird cries, bleats, chatterings, perhaps the thumping splash of a beaver tail on water, then another period of silence.

It doesn't take much. Merely looking up towards the treetops can be enough to trigger the alarm. For many years my favorite duck hunting guide in South Carolina was a black man who had all the attributes of an Indian scout and could call ducks in from a half mile away, just like turning on a magnet. It used to annoy me that he could stand up in the duck blink tootling away and the birds would come right at us, but the moment I stood up to take a shot, they would veer off and depart using the mallard equivalent of full afterburner. Then Johnny told me matter-of-factly one time while scanning the horizon as I crouched in the blind, that it was because my white face flashed a warning, whereas his did not. The next morning I blackened my face with some burnt cork I had prepared in the kitchen of the hunting lodge which seemed to be a good idea until Johnny called me "Mr. Jolson" a couple of times. Next trip I used black and green theatrical makeup to hide my epithelian heliograph, but of late I have used a simple face covering toque, which is easier to remove. In any event, looking up quickly can put wildlife on the alert.

The most productive style of hunting is simply sitting still in one place, preferably within range of a game trail near a watering place, a technique known as "still hunting," and waiting. Navigating one's way carefully, and blazing the trail along the way, one can remain quiet long enough sitting with his back against a tree that the "wilderness alert" will subside and game will again be on the move. Animals, like all of us, tend to follow a route that has been broken by someone previously, so as one proceeds through wild brush and undergrowth he will see clearly marked pathways created by animals passing back and forth over them on a regular basis usually to and from a water hole. These are, of course, the game trails that are most productive hunting spots.

Still hunting is particularly fruitful in the early morning or the late afternoon, when diurnal and nocturnal animals are changing shifts, so to speak, but the timing raises the navigation-on-foot problem enormously. It is recommended that a novice in the woods plan to hunt in the morning so that he will have all day to find his way back to camp and prepare the game for cooking. Once the sun sets, so that one cannot see clearly without an artificial light, it becomes virtually impossible to pick one's way accurately, and being lost in the woods, far from fire and shelter (and the tools to create them), and the water supply of the base camp is a lonely, scary feeling indeed. Also very humbling.

When you do finally see the game of your dreams, don't count too much on dropping it, no matter how much practicing you have done at the rifle range. Another psychological barrier that non-hunters are seldom aware of is called "buck fever," and you will probably be a victim of it.

Buck fever is a condition that can strike any hunter, no matter how experienced, at any time. It usually develops after he has been on the trail for several days without success when suddenly his quarry, say, a large buck deer appears, with which the hunter makes a complete ass of himself by beginning to quake and shake with excitement and promptly rips off a fusillade, totally missing the target. Once, I watched a moose hunter work the reloading lever on a Model '86 Winchester until he emptied the magazine, without firing a shot. He just kept working the lever without ever pulling the trigger until the immense critter gave him a funny look and ambled off into the woods. The guy was so mad that he gave me the rifle, a .33 Winchester, then and there. I still have it.

Bird Hunting

Many upland birds, pheasant, quail, partridge, dove and, in the north country, ptarmigan can be found roosting in heavy cover or feeding either on the ground or in trees. In their wild state most of these birds will not fly far even after a woods alert has sounded, unless actively pursued by a predator. Even then they will frequently move just far enough to escape the danger as they perceive it. The trick is to get in close enough to make a sure kill without scaring them, which requires another stealthy approach. Some birds have developed the defense mechanism of remaining completely motion-less and depend on their natural coloration to camouflage them from view, so that they can be taken with slingshots or sticks.

Migratory birds, particularly ducks and geese, are somewhat more difficult to approach closely and will jump off and fly away if alarmed for any reason. However if a "raft" of waterfowl can be approached by stealth, many can be taken by either a shotgun or a .22 repeating rifle while they are resting on the water (and sometimes may be shot when eating on dry land). Again, in all of these game killing situations, we are not interested in sportsmanship or wingshooting. We are talking about gathering food as a necessity in a survival situation, and a downed airman stranded in the wilderness cannot afford to waste precious, irreplaceable ammunition. He has to make every shot count, if at all possible.

Practice

If you do acquire a survival gun, I repeat: take it out and shoot it, practicing for the time your life may depend on it. Rather than doing all of your shooting at a round bullseye target, buy or make your own silhouette targets of various game animals and practice to see if you can hit squirrels and rabbits in the head consistently. Shoot at realistic ranges and learn your limitations and those of your gun. Shoot in all sorts of light conditions and develop a confident feel for the survival weapon. When you have it, you will be away ahead of the guy who has to depend on snares, traps and sets to put meat on the table.

Preparing Fish and Small Game

One cannot help wondering how many anti-hunting fanatics may be flying their own airplanes and therefore may come face to face with the problems of wilderness survival, particularly the subject of the acquisition and preparation of fish and game. It will be required that such people, who apparently procure their food from the local supermarket already prepared for popping into the oven (or toaster oven), learn how to clean fish and fowl, including birds, squirrels, rabbits and other small game up to and possibly including small deer, so that the edible meat will not become spoiled or tainted.

Before wild game, whether it be fish, bird or animal life, can be consumed, it must normally be cooked, for two reasons. First, is possibility that wildlife may be infested with tapeworms, flukes or other parasites or disease, so it is inadvisable to eat any fish or game raw, no matter where it is taken—unless cooking is simply impossible, as in a life raft. Second, as a practical matter because wild life has a strong "gamey" flavor it usually has to be well cooked in order to be palatable to anyone who has not developed a taste for it. It goes without saying, of course, that game should always be cooked as soon as possible after it is killed. But first, it must be "dressed" (which is a euphemism for cleaned) to avoid any possibility of food poisoning.

All birds (doves, railbirds, grouse) and animals (squirrels, rabbits) can be cleaned immediately in the field. Small birds can be skinned by one's bare hands merely by breaking the skin over the breastbone with pressure of both thumbs simultaneously then more or less peeling it off by working the thumbs all around, but skinning larger birds may require the use of a sharp knife. In the case of fish-eating birds such as seagulls or some types of ducks it is advisable to remove the skin entirely to remove most of the excessively fishy taste. But other avian life, which subsists on grain and corn, especially when larger in the body, should be plucked and after the feathers have been removed prepared with the skin on, as in chickens and turkeys from the supermarket back home.

Cleaning Procedures

Cleaning (or "dressing") game is fundamentally a simple operation, but the sight may come as a surprise to anyone who has never cleaned anything but the icebox. Generally it involves removing the viscera by cutting it off at both ends—the esophagus and the anus—then carefully cutting away the connective tissue so that the entire digestive tract can be removed as a unit. Handle the entrails carefully so as to prevent breakage or spillage which can taint the edible meat; the gall bladder in birds is especially to be handled very gently, since it is delicate.

Filets of fish can be cooked by pinning them to a slab of wood before an open fire.

Small animals are cleaned the same way and should be skinned after evisceration. It is also necessary to remove carefully the musk glands of certain animals to prevent spoilage of edible meat because of the acrid nature of the animals' defensive secretions. Musk glands are found in beaver, opossum, woodchuck, raccoon, rabbit, squirrel, hare, muskrat and (of course) skunk. Rabbits may also have a disease called tularemia, so that great care must be exercised in handling them; gloves are recommended. And in warm weather, rabbits frequently develop tapeworms and other parasites, for which they should be examined in the cleaning process. Remember that young birds and animals tend to spoil more quickly than older ones.

The best way to learn to dress freshly killed game and to locate, identify and excise those pesky musk glands is to go out a few times on hunts in the field with someone during the small-game season and watch him do it, then do it yourself. My late father-in-law, a devotee of the out-of-doors, could clean a fish, a rabbit or a squirrel in ten seconds using his razor sharp pocket knife which included a small gut hook. All it took was three quick cuts and a flip of the wrist. When I try it, I usually wind up with some of the ejecta on my clothing. It takes practice.

Large Animals

Using a .22 rifle or a small gauge shotgun (.410 to 16 gauge) the probability is that your game gathering will be restricted to the small varieties listed above. But if you have a more powerful firearm, such as a .30 caliber rifle, a .357 or .44 Magnum pistol or a 12 gauge shotgun (with size "0" buckshot or rifled slugs) you may be able to collect larger game, such as deer. Venison produces about 570 calories per pound and a lot of it comes in one package, as it were.

Dressing-out larger animals may require larger knives, up to and including a cleaver, to cut through the sternum to open up the rib cage; a hand axe or a machette (carefully wielded!) will act as a cleaver, but my wife's idea about the heavy-duty garden shears— the tool she likes for gathering kindling and clearing brush—would seem to come into good use here, too.

Deer-sized and larger animals (moose, elk, bear) usually are best handled when suspended above the ground to perform the cleaning operation. There are two ways of doing this; both begin by slitting the flesh of the back legs around the "elbow" thus creating a hole between the bone and the heavy tendon (I believe it is comparable to the Achilles tendon at the rear of our ankles), then thrusting a heavy pole through and lifting the carcass so that it is suspended head down. While it is in this position the large blood vessel, or vein in the neck—the jugular—should be slit so that the animal will bleed out freely, which will preserve the meat—and its taste. At this point many experienced hunters recommend that the animal be reversed to a head-up position for the cleaning operation. In the case of antlered animals this may be indicated, but it is cumbersome to do it with any other kind.

Dressing-out is the same as in the case of small game, only on a much larger scale: slit the body from anus to throat, tie off the ends of the digestive tract and remove it, being careful not to spill any of the contents. It may take some careful cutting away of internal membranes as you proceed, using a sharp knife, usually with a short, stout blade. Larger animals also yield such edibles as kidneys and a liver sufficiently large to produce a couple of meals. Liver is loaded with vitamins and iron, but wildlife liver can sometimes be too rich for a city person's consumption. Once the carcass has been cleaned, it should be propped open so that air can enter to cool it out, then it should be wiped with a clean dry cloth or with dead, dry grass. Don't wash it with water; it can induce bacterial action and spoilage will result. The game, once cooled, is then ready for field butchering, which means only that it can be cut into sizes that are manageable to handle for cooking and storing. One last warning: perform the cleaning operation as far from your camp as possible and bury all of the parts you have disposed of. Nothing attracts carnivores and scavengers like the smell of blood and an easy meal. You don't want to have them eyeing you as a possible dessert.

Butchering

Wild game characteristically takes on the flavor of its normal diet and invariably has a stronger taste than what most of us are used to. In the case of larger animals, especially older ones, the more tender cuts of meat (muscle) come from the back, behind the shoulder and from the flanks, with the leg, neck and shoulder muscles being appreciably tougher. Of course, before it can be butchered, the animal must be skinned, another time-consuming process involving the use of a sharp knife and rolled-up sleeves. The hide is slowly peeled with constant tiny passes of the point of the knife blade until it all comes off in one piece. Skinning requires disjointing the animal at the legs and (usually) removing the head, all of which must be also buried under a layer of earth some distance from camp. Preserving the hide requires more equipment and material than anyone in a survival situation will have available, although if you are rescued soon enough afterwards you may be able to retrieve it and have someone make you a bearskin rug or a deerskin pair of gloves and a shirt.

Once all of that has been done, one can begin the job of removing meat for the menu, using the keen edged cutting tool that was involved in all of the procedures so far. Short of going to a packing house and seeing how large animals are butchered by experts, there is no way to learn the butcher's art, not from a book, certainly. So the wilderness survivor will probably hack away at the animal and make a mess of it. Nevertheless, it is edible and will keep him/her alive until help arrives, which is the point of the whole exercise.

Cooking in the Wilds

If you have a large enough container and sufficient water available locally, the easiest way to prepare meat is by boiling, which does not require any culinary expertise. Boiling does not always produce the optimum flavor, but it has the compensating factor of killing most disease bugs, which must be considered whenever anyone is far from real medical care. All that is necessary is to cut the meat into bite-sized chunks (maybe "inch-sized" sounds better drop it into the water container which is hung or propped over a wood fire and wait until it bubbles and boils for a half hour or so. Not only will the meat be edible and chewable, but the broth resulting will be drinkable and nutritious as well, so there will be no waste. And the broth will supply part of your daily requirement for liquid. It doesn't have to be just plain water.

Water containers do not have to be actual pots. With ingenuity and a couple of tools, pieces of the airplane may be shaped into forms that will do the job: a while back we discussed the fellow who used the cowling of his Bonanza as a cooking pot and the squiggly-metal seat supports of his airplane seat as a grill. Having the tool is the secret; that is why we include a pair of metal shears in our survival kit.

With No Pot to Put Water In

If you go down in an all-plastic airplane or one that is fabric covered and no pot-making improvisation is possible (not even from fuel tanks), remember that just about all kinds of meat and fish can be cooked by broiling or roasting if cut to a proper size first. Remember those shish kebabs on the back patio last summer? One of the easiest ways to cook little pieces of meat is simply to impale it on a green stick and hang it over an open fire, merely rotating it from time to

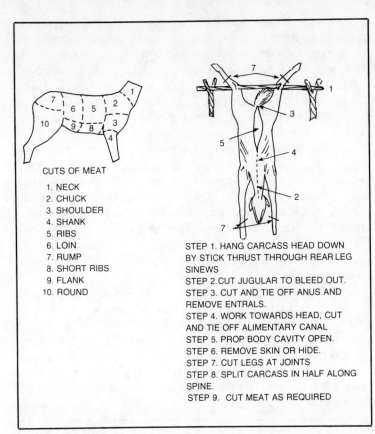

CUTS OF MEAT

1. NECK
2. CHUCK
3. SHOULDER
4. SHANK
5. RIBS
6. LOIN
7. RUMP
8. SHORT RIBS
9. FLANK
10. ROUND

STEP 1. HANG CARCASS HEAD DOWN
BY STICK THRUST THROUGH REAR LEG
SINEWS
STEP 2. CUT JUGULAR TO BLEED OUT.
STEP 3. CUT AND TIE OFF ANUS AND
REMOVE ENTRALS.
STEP 4. WORK TOWARDS HEAD, CUT
AND TIE OFF ALIMENTARY CANAL
STEP 5. PROP BODY CAVITY OPEN.
STEP 6. REMOVE SKIN OR HIDE.
STEP 7. CUT LEGS AT JOINTS
STEP 8. SPLIT CARCASS IN HALF ALONG
SPINE.
STEP 9. CUT MEAT AS REQUIRED

Preparing large game.

time for even exposure to the heat. Small birds can be done the same way. Meat can be cut into thin slices and fish can be filleted and pinned to a piece of log close to the fire until cooked through. How to pin them? Remember the nails in our survival kit?

Aluminum Foil

Few things in our modern civilization have as much all-around utility as heavy duty aluminum foil, readily obtainable at almost any food store or supermarket. Flexible, bendable and tough, heavy duty aluminum foil can be fashioned into drinking cups, cooking pots, drying pans, ovens and roasters. It can be stretched across the face of a reflector fire before a lean-to and will substantially increase the amount of radiant heat reflected into the sleeping area and can be waved in sheets five or six feet long as a recognition signal which in bright sunlight will shimmer and sparkle brightly.

Early-day hunters learned to cook game in the hot coals of their campfires by wrapping it in leaves or a layer of damp clay, but simply wrapping it in aluminum foil will do the job just as well—even better, for no washing of the food is required before eating it. Aluminum foil makes it possible to fry, steam broil (and my wife even braises) meat wrapped in it, and of course any vegetables can be cooked in it, too. Formed into a pot shape, it can be used to boil water and make tea or coffee—or hot chocolate.

Use a piece of foil large enough to wrap the piece of meat, fish, with the shiny side *in*, which makes it more effective. If the meat or vegetable is for some reason on the dry side, add a half ounce or a few spoonsful of water, then align the two edges of the foil and make a series of fold-overs about a half inch or so wide until the foil is snugged over the food, then close the open ends in the same way. Placed in the hot coals for a few minutes, turned once in a while to prevent overcooked spots, will produce a well cooked fish, piece of meat or what have you.

I believe that heavy duty aluminum foil is virtually indispensable in any survival kit and that one can never have too much of it. Frankly, I feel that the small packets of foil (not all of it is heavy duty, either) included in some survival kits is inadequate for any serious survival purpose. It is comparable with the four pieces of bathroom tissue that is also included in such kits. It may be there, but if you really need it, it won't be there long. It is always better to have too much and not need it.

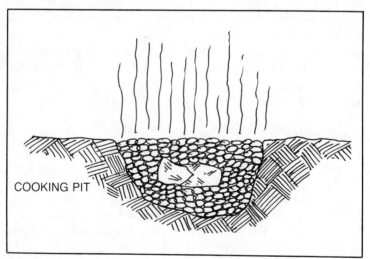

COOKING PIT

Small game can be wrapped in aluminum foil and baked in hot coals placed in a small trench dug in the vicinity of the campfire.

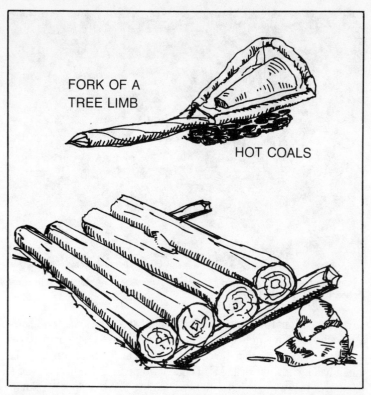

FORK OF A TREE LIMB

HOT COALS

Heavy duty aluminum foil can be used to form pots, dishes, cups or frying pans as illustrated.

Survival Knives

Men who make their living in the woods claim that the knives which they carry constantly are almost as important to them as tools as are the axes they sharpen so meticulously every night. Working knives are not mere decorations on their hips, to be used for such mundane things as opening letters or paring their fingernails. It soon becomes apparent that their knives are stoutly built, but not large. The Maine guide who introduced me to the Savage "Game Getter" shotgun confided over a cup of coffee that he could just about assess a client's experience in the woods by the size of the sheath knife on his belt. His conclusion was, from the experience of many years of experience with hunters, that the larger the knife, the greener the tenderfoot because—he said—every city slicker harbors a secret dream of overcoming a bear in a hand to hand struggle, using his sheath knife. This may account for the large volume of sales of "surplus Marine fighting" (or "combat," or "jungle") knives, some

A popular pocket knife among outdoorsmen is the Buck Lancer, less than three inches long. Courtesy Eddie Bauer, Inc.

with blades eight to ten inches which would make the knife ten inches over-all and I have noticed that most of my wood-wise companions use blades no longer than three and a half inches with knives only six and a half inches over-all. My frequent companion afield, my wife's late father, always carried with him a folding-blade or "pocket" knife which he called a "bird knife", although he used it on other types of game, including fish. It had a three inch razor-sharp blade on one end and a bent-wire of heavy gauge on the other, a "gut" hook for removing entrails cleanly and easily in the field, or on the edge of a stream. I believe that he got it from L. L. Bean in Freeport, Maine.

We have two knives in our hunting (and carry them also in our survival) kit. One is called a "Survival Knife" and has a five and a half inch blade, weighs a mere ten ounces and has a recess in its handle for some monofilament, some hooks and a few waterproofed matches. The other knife, which I usually drop into my pocket when off fishing (along with my match-safe, plumber's candle, magnifying glass, signalling mirror, smoke generator and police whistle) has a three and a half inch folding blade and weighs a mere seven and a half ounces. Both knives are by Smith & Wesson.

...And Sharpening Them

A dull knife is an abomination. To be useful in the field the blade should literally be razor sharp, sharp enough to cut a page of a

122

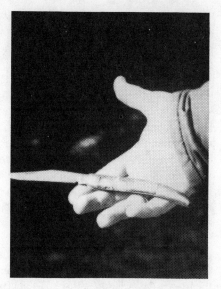

A folding knife that has been the author's regular companion afield for many years for cleaning small game and fish immediately as it is taken. A heavy belt-knife is not necessary for most purposes.

newspaper dropped lengthwise on it; sharp enough to shave with. With such a blade, cutting fuzz sticks or cleaning game or slicing food is a pleasure. But the cutting edge must be sharpened and then kept sharp. When you purchase a knife, also buy a blade sharpening outfit which consists of a sharpening stone and sharpening oil.

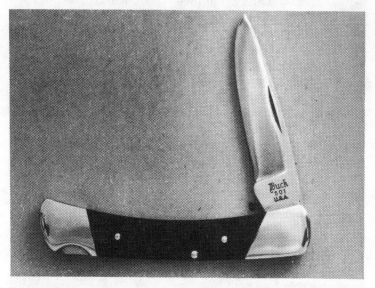

The Buck Esquire knife is a sturdy, all-purpose cutting tool made of high-carbon 440 tool steel. It measures 3¾ inches closed, and 6½ inches open. Courtesy Eddie Bauer, Inc.

As in the remarks about cleaning game, we can tell you how to do a job of sharpening your knife, but it is far better to have someone show you how to do it and be sure that you are doing it right, not ruining the cutting edge.

The technique is to flow sharpening oil on the stone so that the particles of grit and steel will float away from the contact area and not scar the delicate cutting edge, which looks almost lace-like under a high-resolution microscope. Lay the blade flat on the face of the stone, then raise the back of the blade slightly and draw the blade lightly-but-firmly across the oiled surface in what might be described as a "shaving motion," alternating the blade on each stroke so as to keep the sharpening balanced on both sides of the edge—and remembering to keep the angle of the blade to the stone constant. After a dozen or so strokes, wipe the blade clean and then run the blade across a piece of leather in just the opposite of the shaving direction, to smooth out the fine edge, a function known as "stropping". I use my boots or a leather belt most of the time. A few minutes a day will keep the knife sharp enough to split a hair.

An Alternative Approach

There is no reason for a lightplane occupant ever having to prepare to eat grubs, worms, berries and lizards, *if* one plans ahead for the *possibility* of ever having to set 'er down out in the boondocks, summer or winter. It doesn't take a great deal of planning, either, for a tremendous assortment of food is readily available in forms that are light, compact, easily prepared and relatively inexpensive. You don't even have to be a competent cook.

Seasoned campers know all sorts of ways to prepare meals afield on minimum equipment, including baking, broiling, braising, barbequeing frying, roasting and stewing. But campers set out intending to rough it, so, particularly if travelling by automobile, camper, or by canoe or burro, carry their own preparations and equipment along: flour, salt, sugar, hamburgers, eggs, chicken, fresh fruits, vegetables and all sorts of pots, pans and utensils—including multi-burner camp stoves. Backpackers tote less, but also set off prepared to spend some time in the brush. So, it can be done. There is no excuse for not taking along in our airplane a couple of weeks' worth of nutritional and good-tasting food that will keep us well fed and happy—and healthy.

Reconstitutable Foods

The technique of dehydrating some foods was discovered many years ago—anyone over the age of 20 must remember Arthur

Godfrey selling "Lipton's Noodle Soup in a Bag"; he pronounced it "noooodle" —and of course tea bags, Lipton's and others, have been around for many moons.

In the last 20 years, an enormous industry has developed in the realm of quick-foods, many of which can be purchased at the local supermarket and many others, which can be obtained from outdoors suppliers and sporting goods stores and nationally known outdoors outfitters, like Eddie Bauer, L. L. Bean, Norm Thompson, Gokey, Orvis and both boating (e.g.: Chris Craft) and aviation (Sporty's Pilot Shop) mail order supply houses.

Remember that a total of five gallons of water will supply the requirements of two people for a week. If four of the required six "glasses" (i.e.: half pints) of liquid can be used to reconstitute the packets of dehydrated or freeze-dried food, it would mean that you could prepare a varied menu of 28 meals (for two people, it would take 56 of the food packets). Although you might elect, as we do, to carry 75 or 100 packets, without water available, they are unpreparable and inedible. *Never* eat reconstitutable foods straight out of the packets.

However, if you have a good local source and supply of fresh water, you may be able to live—or at least eat—pretty well for a couple of weeks, courtesy of modern science.

Most of these reconstitutable foods come in plastic or metal-foil envelopes about 4-1/2″ × 6″ × 1/2″ thick and contain everything from—literally—soup to nuts. Just running my eye over a bunch of them piled on the table next to my typewriter I see vegetable stew, scrambled eggs mix, meat balls, beef stew, cheese omelette, macaroni and cheese, beef and rice, potato casserole and a wide variety of soups, beverages and desserts. My wife includes powdered milk, which can be reconstituted by water, then adds powdered "Instant Breakfast" which comes in several flavors, including chocolate and strawberry. She also uses the instant milk (reconstituted) to hype-up the dehydrated mashed potatoes. I might add that she takes along baggies of sugar, and salt and pepper in little waterproof shakers.

There are also some reconstitutable meals which are contained in their own cups, which contain noodles mixed with pork, beef, chicken, beef and chicken, and shrimp. They are a little bulky for a survival kit, but there is no reason why they could not be stowed in the baggage compartment.

There are also commercially available jerky, bacon bars, tropical chocolate, trail cookies, raisins and assorted nuts, all packaged in waterproof plastic packages. The list is almost endless and certainly a 100 meal menu for a full month's stay, with all sorts of taste varieties. Preparing for a two week stay should be easy. And for a week, elementary. All it takes is 21 packets, a pot, some water and a folding stove and you can eat pretty well.

Of course, we always have some extra food along for socializing. Along with a couple of pretty bottles in what looks like a typewriter case, we have a couple of cans of sardines, some saltines and a bar or two of sharp cheese, all of which may serve to keep body and soul together under certain circumstances.

At the end of last summer's boating season, two of our friends sailed the Chesapeake for two weeks in a 36′ sailboat, without touching land. During that period they lived on the food in their survival kit and, although it was more than a year old, reported that their meals were satisfying and delicious. Which is a pretty good report on the usefulness of reconstitutable foods. It's a damsite better than eating bark.

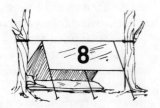

Our Survival Kit

Let me start off by saying that there is too much glamour in the term "survival kit," What we are talking about is equipping ourselves ahead of time for an encounter with a potential hazard. It does not apply *only* to flying, or to being lost in the woods while hunting or having a bush pilot fly off and forget where he left you.

As a practical matter, many of us who drive cars in the wintertime when it is bitterly cold—whether snow is on the ground or in the offing— carry "survival" equipment in the trunks of our family cars. Few of us would think of going off on a trip without a spare tire, a jack and lug wrench, although flat tires are pretty much of a rarity nowadays. In addition, we carry a broom, a folding shovel, anti-skid chains, a steel tow-cable, a set of battery-jumping cables, police-type red fusees that will indicate a problem by burning brightly in red for an hour or two, and warning reflector-signs. In addition, since normal street clothing would be so inappropriate for changing a tire or digging out of a snow bank, we may toss in thermal coveralls, woolen socks and thermal boots, heavy work gloves and a furlined hat with ear coverings. No one may think of that as a survival kit, but that is what it is. A couple of years back we were given an emergency first aid kit for our car, all self contained in what looks like a businessman's portfolio or a seat cushion, for it is lined with foam rubber. It contains bandages, ointments, surgical scissors, a space blanket and a dayglow-marked sash that can be worn across the body or waved like a warning flag. That, too, is now a part of our automobile survival kit.

127

Aircraft Survival Kits—Generally

Don't let the term survival kit throw you. What we are going to try to do, remember, is—having examined the problems of survival in the wilderness in a variety of circumstances—provide a means of coping with them until someone comes and gets us. There is no perfect list of contents for a survival kit that will meet every need, but a well planned equipment list can be created to meet most survival requirements. There must always be a certain number of trade-offs, a careful balancing of gotta-haves vs. like-to-haves with an eye to weight, bulk and portability—i.e.: How quickly can you get out of the airplane with it?

It may be that your needs will be adequately served by any one or more of the kits that can be purchased over the counter or by mail order. Indeed one supplier, Nicolet Products, is so confident in its product that guarantees buyers will like it, and if they don't, they will get a full refund. However, we caution you to consider the adequacy of *any* kit, including ours, to meet the *worst* situation *you* might possibly encounter. After all, once you are down, you can't go back and pick up the items you don't have. The four most worthless things to aviators are,

> The Sky Above You
> The Runway Behind You
> The Fuel Still in the Ground, and for downed airmen,
> The Survival Kit Back in the Attic

The Fair Weather Survival Kit

Back in Chapter 2 we told about our basic "Grab Bag", or grab-it-and-get-out Bag, the contents of which should get us through a few days in warm climate. But what about special problems: winter in the mountains or summer on the desert, or going down at sea? No one kit could fill the bill for all of the places that we fly in the course of the year. What we needed was sort of a portable automobile trunk that we could repack as the requirements changed. We figured that equipment that would keep us alive in freezing weather was what was needed and we could work backwards from that.

Our Big Red Bag

We began by laying the things we thought we needed on the floor of our living room, divided into sections: "Must Have," "Should Have," "Nice to Have," "Only if We Have Space," then subdivided into Shelter, Fire and Food. It did not take very long to see that the Eddie Bauer 18-1/2″ long carryall bag was not going to be large

The author on his way to Buffalo, NY in January. The airline-type Grab Bag in left hand, and the Big Red Bag in right. Too much survival equipment for a two-hour flight? Not for FKS!

enough. In the attic, where I keep my fishing equipment, was a large red Scuba diver's carry-all, in which I had my wet suit, regulator, a medium sized air tank, weights, snorkels, face masks and flippers, all of which was soon dumped out so we could see if that would carry the survival equipment piled up around the coffee table.

I recalled seeing a bag about that size—30″ long and 13″ in diameter—on the back seat of a floatplane on North Bay, in Ontario and it just struck me what that bag really was.

The selections were not as difficult as we had thought. Since we dress according to the weather anyhow, we assumed that we would be wearing cold weather outfits in the wintertime, including winter underwear, down-filled jackets, hats and gloves, and of course less clothing as the weather grew milder. We also keep some equipment in the plane: a machette, some fishing gear and foul-weather gear. The inventory we wound up with in our Big Red Bag looked something like this:

Shelter and Protection
3 plastic tarpaulins 9″ × 12″
2 sets of waffle-weave underwear
2 medium weight wool shirts
2 heavy weight wool shirts
2 nylon shell wind-breakers

```
4  pairs of wool socks
2  pairs of rubber galoshes
2  pairs of work gloves (which fit into...
2  pairs of leather mittens
1  mummy-type sleeping bag (only one person can sleep at a time)
1  take-down crosscut saw
1  12 gauge repeating shotgun with 50 rounds of assorted
   ammo
1  AR-7 Survival Rifle
```

Fire Making

```
1000 waterproofed wooden matches, distributed in pack
several pads of fine-grade steel wool
several plumbers candles and self-relighting candles
1  cruising axe
2  cricket-type cigarette lighters
1  pair long handled heavy-duty tree pruning shears
```

(we also carry magnifying glasses, signalling mirrors, police whistles, plumbers candles and matches on our person.)

Food Supply and Preparation

75 foil packets of reconstitutable food, removed from their boxes and spread through the layers of clothing. A box of 12 packets measures approximately $6'' \times 7'' \times 4''$ or 168 cu. in., so that 72 packets in their cardboard boxes take up more than one-fourth of the available space. However, from those boxes and packed individually, we have no trouble putting more than three weeks' worth of such food into the bag. We won't go into the individual contents, for we try to vary the menu available. You can check with your local supermarket and sporting goods and boat supply stores.

```
2  rolls of heavy duty aluminum foil (also removed from their boxes)
1  pair of heavy-duty kitchen scissors
2  Sterno alcohol-burning collapsible stoves  (and)
4  cans of Sterno
4  previously prepared cooking candles ("buddy burners")
2  sets of eating implements (knife, fork, spoon)
1  set or removable-handle nesting pots (sauce pans) from six cup
   to four cup to three cup sizes, with
1  demountable fishing rod, with reel and assorted hooks/ lures
1  cooking grate, round (12'' across, of heavy gauge wire)
```

Miscellaneous Items for Comfort and Hygiene

1   100 foot ball of light twine
1   dozen ten-penny nails
1   sewing kit with extra buttons in various sizes
2   rolls of toilet paper
1   folding shovel
2   towels
2   wash rags
1   box Ivory Snow
2   bars of soap (hotel size)
1   a pack of safety pins
2   military style web belts
2   military type canteens in holders (with canteen cups)
1   pair sheet metal shears

Discovery Aids

2   dayglow hunters' vests
1   flare pistol
2   strobe lights (rescue type)
1   Japanese kite with a *long* silvery mylar tail (it can be seen for 20 miles in bright sun!)
1   "personnel-type" emergency locator beacon—That's right, we have *three* of them, in case we get separated.

Eddie Bauer's Big Bag. Made from Cordura, a sturdy nylon duck treated with urethane to repel water and resist stains. It is 30 inches long and 13 inches in diameter and ideal for packing survival gear.

A variety of gear and duffle bags from Eddie Bauer, Seattle, WA. Made of heavy duty 22-ounce canvas duck, any of these are useful for transporting survival gear. They range in size from 20″ × 9½″ × 11½″ to 34″ × 14″ the latter being large enough to contain a sleeping bag.

Note what I said about our normally worn very cold weather down-filled jackets. These are so attractively designed now that we wear them all winter and therefore count on having them in the cabin with us, not only the jackets but the quick-on-and-off quilted (down filled) warm-up or Himalayan type winter trousers, and Eddie Bauer down-filled hats and face masks.

Coupled with the contents of the Grab Bag, our fair weather basic kit, the Red Bag, fully packed, will support two people for two weeks IF there is sufficient water to reconstitute the freeze-dried or dehydrated foods. However, if all five gallons that we try to carry are available in the four one-gallon containers and the four canteens, i.e.: if they are not broken or otherwise lost in the accident or by freezing, splitting the jugs, then leaking away, we have *six* full days of pre-pared food "useable," as the saying goes. The survival rifle and the shotgun may be our tickets to survival. Of course, if water is nearby, the situation will be better.

Although its weight varies with the time of year to cope with any seasonal changes, the Red Bag grosses out at about 50 pounds, maximum, which seems a lot less under conditions of stress; it is amazing how strong one becomes when adrenalin starts flowing. We know that we are not carrying a suite at the Ritz along in our Big Red Bag, but are confident that our rescuers will find us "physically unharmed, died of exposure". And, as the saying goes, That's the name of *that* game.

How About Walking Out?

The psychological drive to "do something" is very strong in anyone who has been raised on our fast-paced modern society, hence there is a natural tendency for anyone who is for some reason displaced from it to want to take some affirmative action to return to civilization.

The Natural Urge to "Do Something"

This is a common experience for city-bred people who are for some reason off in wild country—for hunting, fishing or hiking, say—and become disoriented. It is a particularly scary feeling when the lost person is caught by an early sunset, for it tends to get very dark in the woods long before the sky has lost all of its twilight. Woodsmen have an old trick to keep them from making their condition worse if and when (more likely *when*, because anyone *can*) they become completely confused in the forest, particularly in snowy conditions. They pick one tree and walk around it *all night,* never taking the chance of going to sleep without adequate protection from the chill. The reason for doing this is that a situation can be made immeasurably worse if one wanders so far off that a search party cannot even guess where he might be. And if one falls at night and is hurt enough not to be able to keep moving, even with a sprain or strain, and much worse if suffering from a fracture, it can be fatal in many cases. I know of a hunter in northern Maine who propped his rifle against a tree; then climbed another tree to find his bearings and never found the rifle again.

Avoiding the Problem in the First Place

In flying lingo "IFR" means Instrument Flight Rules, but it can also mean "I Follow Roads". When contemplating a flight across rough or obviously forbidding territory, such as the Western Deserts, Death Valley, passes through the Rocky Mountains or the Appalachian Range, we plan our route with an eye to the sprawling Interstate Highway system and always plan to fly over such routes in good weather. Although filing a Visual Flight Plan giving a routing such as "Oklahoma City to Albuquerque via Route 66", or "Cheyenne to San Francisco via Ogden and Interstate 80" may sound peculiar, it is comforting to look down on those long ribbons of concrete and know that, even while crossing the most craggy or harsh terrain, if we do have to make an unplanned landing, we *can* walk for help to a form of civilization, on wheels.

A Daniel Boone, You Ain't

However, let us assume that our point of unintended arrival is not close to any highways, railroads, communities or other sources of immediate help. We are on our own, for a while at least. Now what?

If we have prepared ahead of time to cope with the emergency, we will have at the landing (I hate the word "crash") site the necessary life support system—survival equipment—to keep us going for a week or so. Reviewing the size and weight of that inventory will make it abundantly clear that for most people, who in this Age of the Internal Combustion Engine are not in very good physical condition, adequate survival/support equipment is too heavy and too bulky to carry. Unless one is well conditioned and experienced in the lore of backpack camping, he is soon going to find himself unprepared for a personal confrontation with merciless nature. It can indeed be lethal. They call the results, "death due to exposure."

True, under certain conditions trained outdoorsmen can survive with minimum equipment, for example, Boy Scouts who have undergone the special living-off-the-land course at the Philmont Scout Ranch in New Mexico or people who have participated in the programs of the group known as "Outward Bound." The graduates of both of these projects can literally survive in the wilderness with no more equipment than a knife. But they are rare individuals, indeed.

Since childhood, reading about the adventures of early backwoodsmen and explorers have stirred our minds with visions of adventure and romance. Who has not imagined setting out on foot from North America's eastern coast as they did and walking westward, across mountains, prairies, fording rivers—equipped with only an axe, a knife, a muzzle loading rifle, a couple of pounds of lead balls, a couple of pounds of black powder, a blanket and the clothes on one's back? Lost in the mists of nostalgia are the incredible hardships they encountered and survived—some of them. Few tales are told about the ones who died of infections, pneumonia, drowning, or of suffering broken bones, which led to their dying of starvation, lying on the hard ground, vulnerable to the attacks of wild animals and hostile natives. Admittedly, some of them did make it. But first of all, when they started, they were tough from the bone out. Second, they were inured to discomforts which they took as a part of their normal lives in the days before steam or electric heat, or indoor plumbing. There is simply no way that any of us can start off from scratch and do what they did in their minimal outfits. This is something to keep in mind when planning a flight.

However, if you have set sail without telling anyone ahead of time—no flight plan, no telephone calls—or have strayed far from your intended route, or are on the ground in a remote area of Canada, Mexico or the United States, you may decide to—or have someone in your party—set out on foot to get help. This must be a judgement made on the basis of the circumstances in which you find yourself and with a clear understanding of some hard facts.

The primary rule, whether you are down in dense woods, craggy mountains or on a broiling desert is *never* start off on foot unless you are absolutely sure that you can reach your destination with the water supply that is available! Rule two is *never* start out on foot unless you are wearing well broken-in hiking shoes, for city-type footwear is totally inadequate for heavy work, and any footwear that causes chafing and blisters creates a serious problem afield. You will also need a pack containing shelter, foul weather gear, basic first aid materials and fire making equipment, as well as signalling devices, a wood-cutting implement (saw, axe, machette) and possibly a survival weapon, all of which will weigh about 30 pounds. Rule three is that, before starting out, you must know your location with reasonable precision and the direction and best route to civilization. This means that you must have an accurate terrain map (World Air Charts won't be much good for this because their scale is too small and details scanty) which shows streams, swampy areas, mud flats, hills, valleys and rivers. A good quality woods-cruiser compass will be required for navigating in the bush, too.

Hearken to the wise words of Yogi Berra who once said: "If you don't know where you are going, you may wind up somewhere else".

The Mechanics of Walking

In order to understand the physical problems of hiking from a remote crash site back to civilization—and by remote I mean at least two days and one overnight in the wilderness, which in rough country is not very many miles—let's take what may be a brand new look at an act we all tend to take for granted.

Walking is a complicated series of physical actions involving balancing, or rather, un-balancing and reacting. On a level surface—floors, hallways, pavements, gold fairways, beaches—a pattern of movements can be discerned. From a position of standing at rest, with the body balanced over its metacenter and center of gravity, walking starts with a slight lean in the direction of motion. If you don't move your feet at all, you will fall over. That is what happens when someone trips or has his foot motion somehow restricted. Having leaned and thereby moved your center of gravity (actually, engineers call this "shifting the metacenter") the next step (literally) is to move a foot out to prevent falling, but instead of merely propping you up, the body moves ahead as its off balance condition continues, with one foot following the other in a series of movements known as taking steps, or walking. But watch the way the feet and legs move. To walk on a smooth surface, the knee is bent just enough for the foot moving forward to clear the surface (actually, it is a complex combination of hip, knee and ankle movements. If a light bulb were affixed to the ankle and a time exposure made the resulting line of light would describe a low undulation. That is how citified people walk from earliest childhood.

Walking the Rough

When a person walks in rough country, whether crossing a plow-furrowed field or one heavily overgrown with brush, the conditions and the style or walking are far different. Instead of the sidewalk-type gliding motion of striding along, each step has another dimension: upwards. An ankle generated line of light would be jagged, sawtoothed, rather than undulant. A person who might normally stride along 30 inches at a time (considered a normal stride by the military) might be shortened to 18 inches in the field. This means that one must take some 3500 higher-than-usual steps to cover a mile—almost twice as many steps as are required to walk a mile in the city or on a golf course. Walking any distance in rough country is tiring. I have seen desk-bound business and professional men after they have spent "opening day" of the small game season walking fields and hedgerows so exhausted that they could not bend their legs to get into their cars to go home. In addition to the pain from using what ordinarily are little-used muscles and the resultant stiffness, be warned that the heavy use of of untrained or out-of-tone muscles can result in excruciating, frequently disabling muscular cramps, particularly if the muscle becomes chilled. Anyone who has undergone the experience of a muscle cramp in a big toe, or foot or calf muscle in the middle of the night can understand the potential pain from a seizure in a huge muscle group like the *Quadraceps extensors* on the front of the thigh (the foot lifting muscles) or the *Biceps flexor cruris* at the rear of the thigh after a full day of traversing rough country.

The situation is worse then in mountainous country, even if the mountains are small when seen from an airplane 8,000 feet high.

Climbing Hills

A small mountain in the Pennsylvania Poconos or the Appalachians only 2,300 feet high—less than half a mile—is the equivalent of a building more than 200 stories high, a hundred yards higher that the twin towers of the World Trade Center in New York City. If normal sized stairs with eight inch risers (the size used in most homes) were affixed to the side of that low mountain, it would require 3065 steps, each lifting the climber's weight (including a pack on his back) straight up. That is not the worst of it. Coming down is more difficult on the legs, the knee and ankle joints and one's insides because of the succession of jolts; did you ever notice how you can go up steps more smoothly than coming down? And walking up and down mountain trails is much more tiring and hazardous than mounting or descending a flight of stairs. Doing it without any trail to guide you makes it even more difficult and more dangerous. All it takes is one sprained ankle...

Other Hazards on the Trail

In the section on hunting we discussed the inherent problem of hunters leaving camp and becoming lost and not being able to find the base camp again, a set of circumstances that is commonly encountered any time one's landmark orientation is lost. Oil rig workers in Alaska tell of fellows who have gone outside in a blizzard to get a breath of fresh air for a few moments and lost their way only 15 or 20 feet from the snow-camouflaged entrance. In the woods, having someone at the base camp who can whistle you in is a help, but a solo camper has to be extra careful whenever departing the immediate vicinity.

138

Intentionally leaving a campsite for the purpose of walking-out creates an ultrahazardous situation for it indicates that you have consciously decided to abandon it as a position of security and an identifiable crash location as seen from the air. No matter what time of the year or the geographic location, you must make yourself understand the possible implications of such a decision so it is not arrived at from panic.

In the best (i.e.: warm climate) situations there will be in most areas all sorts of obstacles to travelling on foot including heavy vegetation, rough terrain, water courses (streams, rivers and lakes), marshy areas (including quicksand), soft or mucky ground totally unfit for overnight camping and very possibly scourges of insects, from mosquitoes to no-see-ums. The risk of an ankle sprain or muscle strain, which is merely an inconvenience back in the city, could seal your fate in the wilderness, especially if your are travelling alone, hence most advisors say never to travel alone if you can avoid it.

It is worse in the wintertime when the air temperature drops below freezing and especially if there is snow on the ground, for a light mantle of drifted snow can hide rocks, uneven ground, streams in what seem to be innocuous little ditches and animal holes. Before embarking on a cross country trek on foot, remember that no survival kit is designed to provide sufficient calories for the amount of effort that will be expended in such an effort and that it is hard when on the move to collect an ample supply of firewood, ignite it and keep it burning enough to warm you and cook your food, it any. Natural foods are hard to find in winter, especially when snow is falling.

The message is clear: under the very best of circumstances, in summertime, it will not be a stroll in the country, but a dangerous journey. Wilderness hiking is a slow, arduous business at best and you cannot cover much ground before you have to begin making preparations for an overnight camping site.

Such a hike obviously is worse and fraught with more dangers and disagreeable consequences when made in winter weather so that making the wrong decision can lead to worsening the situation, not improving it. Remember, first of all that if you do file a flight plan *someone* will know that you are presumed down and the approximate location of your off-airport site so that search and rescue teams will be looking for you in *that* area. Second, remember that they will be looking for an *airplane* on the ground, and you know from your own experience that an object the size of an airplane is easier to spot than a human figure. Furthermore, the close-to-the-airplane campsite will have a number of signalling aids, rather than the one or two you might be able to carry if travelling on foot. If the wreck's radios are operable, that is another big plus factor for ground-to-air communication. If you are unable to speak by radio, you can signal basic information by either signalling panel displays or by well recognized body positions.

And remember also that you will be able to travel only four or five miles *a day* on foot in heavy country, a distance that can be covered in a couple of minutes by a search plane or helicopter. Therefore, the dogma of all search and rescue people is: Don't Move! They recommend that the best course of action is to stay with the airplane and wait to be rescued.

However...

If after two weeks in the wilderness, where your emergency food packets may have run out and there has been no sign of an air search, you may come to the conclusion that it is a choice between getting out on your own two feet or die. It must be that serious before you should seriously consider taking up your bed and walking.

Hopefully, you will have at least minimum survival equipment that can be carried including two quart-sized canteens of fresh water, protection from the elements, bedding—even if only a space blanket and a tube tent-fire-making equipment, a cutting instrument (at least an axe), signalling devices and a survival gun. And well broken-in hiking boots. Not low shoes, as worn in the city, but at least ankle-high hiking boots, designed for heavy duty use. Everyone agrees that proper supportive footgear is the most important piece of equipment for an extended journey on foot and that two pairs of socks should be included. In addition to the hazards of sprained ankles afield, blisters on the foot can be incapacitating and perspiration dampened socks can lead to blisters, so socks should be alternated to keep dry ones or the feet as much as possible. In extremely cold weather, dampness robs socks, even the best quality woolen socks, of their insulating qualities which leads to all kinds of complications including frostbite, which is why the best advice out of Alaska and Canada is not to try to travel in extremely cold weather, but to stay holed up and conserve your strength.

Navigating on Foot

The technique of navigating on foot is no different from setting up any dead reckoning problem, whether in an airplane or a boat. If you know precisely the point from which you start and have a definite destination in mind, you can plan to proceed from one place to the other, rather than just wandering around aimlessly which doesn't accomplish anything. As in planning a cross-country, the first step is to draw a line on the best chart available. Hikers/campers usually use Geological Survey Charts which are on a 1:25,000 scale and show the details of the terrain down to and including small streams, dirt roads and private homes. Obviously, these would be the best for walking-out, but few of us carry a full set around in our airplanes, so we will most likely have to depend on the standard Aeronautical Sectional Chart, drawn on a scale of 1:500,000, which translates to eight miles to the inch. To put it another way, on the hoof, if you can travel 20 miles in the course of a day—which is problematical, as we have discussed before—you will cover about two and a half inches on the Sectional, a distance that takes about ten minutes in a small plane. There are places in the highly populated Eastern Seaboard of the United States where it could take as long as a week of walking-out (note: not just "walking") to reach human contact.

While I am at it, World Aeronautical Charts (WACs) at a scale of 1:1,000,000 are totally worthless for walking-out since they do not contain enough details and are frequently wrong in outside-the-U.S. coverage. Come to think of it, the Sectionals aren't so hot, either, although they will show large features such as major highways, railroad lines, towns and hamlets. However, elevation contour lines spaced at 1,000 feet vertically won't indicate a hill unless it is higher than an 80 story building, which is food for thought when considering laying out a route.

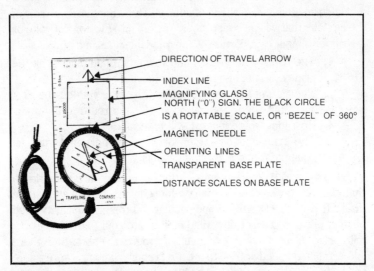

The Silva Travelling Compass.

The Magnetic Compass

There are many types of hand-held magnetic compasses, ranging from brassbound military surplus artillerymens' and surveyers' types to the little dime-sized versions that may be found on the tops of many matchsafes and sometimes in Cracker Jack boxes. I shouldn't make light of the last-named. During the latter days of WWII a friend of mine who was herding a TBM torpedoplane from the Philippines to Iwo Jima all by himself had the somewhat unnerving experience of losing his entire electrical system and having the airplane's wet compass spring a leak all at the same time—at night! Quick thinking saved his bacon: in the survival equipment every Naval Aviator festooned himself with in those days, he had hanging around his neck a match-safe with one of those tiny toy compasses, and damn if he didn't dead-reckon that lumpy airplane across 500 miles of open ocean using only that tiny magnetic needle and his wrist watch, illuminating them every so often with his flashlight.

Some compasses are designed for hunters and campers and have built-in protractor and straightedge and compute the actual magnetic course from true based on local annual variation shown on the chart. The one we favor is the Silva which drops into a shirt pocket and can be attached to our persons by neck lanyards, so it is always handy when in the woods.

Always Leave Notes

Before you set out on any trip on foot, either let someone know what you are going to do ahead of time or leave a note on some part of the airplane that will be conspicuous: tucked into the control yoke or instrument panel or a corner of the windshield telling:

1. The names, addresses and telephone numbers of all the plane's occupants
2. The date of the occurrence and the date you left the site
3. Your intended destination and/or the route to be taken
4. How long you expect it will take, and
5. The type and character of your support and survival equipment and signalling capability

On the trail, take frequent sightings of prominent landmarks so that you will stay on course, every hundred yards or so leave a blaze mark. It doesn't have to be spectacular; a broken branch, twisted bush or pile of stones or dirt will do it indicate your path. And every mile or so, *leave another note* giving a progress report: time there and estimated speed or time to the next reporting point where a note will be left. In this way you will be blazing a trail for any search party that may be looking for you and also to enable you to return to the airplane if you begin to have any second thoughts.

The very term "dead reckoning" (which really is "ded" for "deduced") presupposes one perception of distance covered as well as the direction of travel, so you will have to keep a record of that, too. Distance estimates in the wild are usually made simply by counting steps, say, 100 or so at a time and keeping a record. Although, as previously remarked, the military "normal" stride is 30 inches,

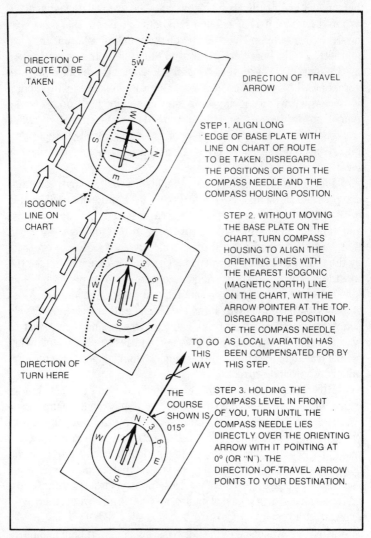

DIRECTION OF ROUTE TO BE TAKEN

5W

DIRECTION OF TRAVEL ARROW

STEP 1. ALIGN LONG EDGE OF BASE PLATE WITH LINE ON CHART OF ROUTE TO BE TAKEN. DISREGARD THE POSITIONS OF BOTH THE COMPASS NEEDLE AND THE COMPASS HOUSING POSITION.

ISOGONIC LINE ON CHART

STEP 2. WITHOUT MOVING THE BASE PLATE ON THE CHART, TURN COMPASS HOUSING TO ALIGN THE ORIENTING LINES WITH THE NEAREST ISOGONIC (MAGNETIC NORTH) LINE ON THE CHART, WITH THE ARROW POINTER AT THE TOP. DISREGARD THE POSITION OF THE COMPASS NEEDLE AS LOCAL VARIATION HAS BEEN COMPENSATED FOR BY THIS STEP.

DIRECTION OF TURN HERE

TO GO THIS WAY

THE COURSE SHOWN IS 015°

STEP 3. HOLDING THE COMPASS LEVEL IN FRONT OF YOU, TURN UNTIL THE COMPASS NEEDLE LIES DIRECTLY OVER THE ORIENTING ARROW WITH IT POINTING AT 0° (OR "N"). THE DIRECTION-OF-TRAVEL ARROW POINTS TO YOUR DESTINATION.

How to Use the Silva Travelling Compass.

which figures out to 2112 steps to cover a mile, it is far more realistic for an out-of-condition civilian, especially if carrying a 30-pound pack on his back, to figure on no more than 14 or 15 inches, which would come out to more like 4,525 (short) steps to cover that distance. And crossing very soft or marshy ground may reduce the stride to a foot or 5,280 steps to go a mile.

For estimating the distance they cover, woodsmen usually keep a record (called a "tally") of each 100 (or 200 or 500) steps taken by tying a slipknot in a length of rawhide fastened to a shirt button—although any string or even a shoelace will do just as well. When the tally cord has enough slipknots to indicate that a mile has been covered (35 or 17 or whatever the number counted) they are unknotted and a knot tied in a second thong, with the original retied as the journey progresses. It seems like an unnecessary chore to someone who can look up at a secret sign and tell where he is, but it is necessary when moving in unfamiliar territory. It doesn't take much effort; there is nothing else to do most of the time while walking but count steps-and-tie knots and occasionally take a sighting on the compass. And it gives at least an approximate idea of one's location.

It is generally recommended that hikers walk around mountains and proceed through passes, keeping to one altitude if possible. It is best to avoid marshes and flooded areas where progress is difficult and camping impossible. When planning to hike out, keep in mind that sometimes the fastest way between two points is not necessarily the most direct way. It will pay off if you plan carefully to take the most level route, one that avoids steep slopes to surmount hills and stay on a trail that offers the least difficult walking conditions. Most streams lead eventually to some kind of habitation and in really wild country well worn animal trails will lead to streams, or at least to water holes. It is considerably easier and less tiring to follow an animal trail than to spend time hacking or plunging headlong through undergrowth and brush.

However, the warning must be repeated: don't get lost! It is an article of faith among woodsmen that when in strange or unfamiliar woods territory they never venture far without a compass, especially when going it alone. Years of woods-lore and experience has taught us that a characteristic of anyone lost in such circumstances and not equipped with a compass is—no matter how good their "sense of direction" —to wander around in a circle and there are many recorded instances of hunters, hikers and woodsmen who expired as a result of exposure because they did so.

Most survival manuals include basic information about finding or determining compass directions by referring to the position of the

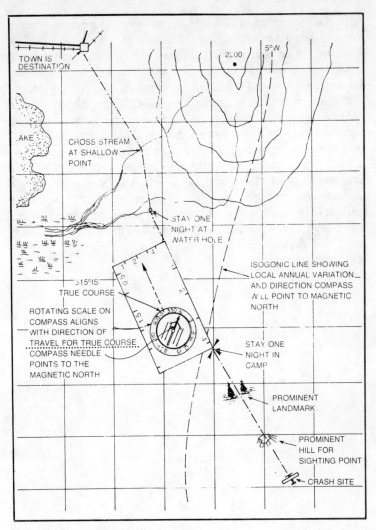

Navigating by the Silva Travelling Compass.

sun in the daytime or the stars at night: how to locate the Big Dipper *(Ursis Major,* to astronomers) and the North Star *(Polaris),* which most children over the age of ten know anyhow. And most people are aware that in North America the sun rises in the east and sets in the west after following an arc towards the south. But just knowing the general direction of the cardinal points is only of momentary assistance and will not prevent the circling tendency, especially if the skies are obscured by cloud cover or heavy forest growth. Furthermore, having at best a vague notion of a compass direction is totally unreliable for doing an accurate job of following a precise course without the guidance of recognized landmarks, whether in a boat far from land or on foot in the wilderness. If you have no survival equipment on board and if no one has any reason to know that you have gone down, and if you have positive knowledge that you are within no more than a day from a settled community and if the weather is not forbidding because of freezing temperature or deep snow or extremely heavy rain which might cause severe flash floods, so that walking-out is feasible after considering all of the possibilities, it is not difficult to remove the magnetic (or "wet") compass from the instrument panel of the airplane to give you basic guidance. Of course, you must also meet the requirements initially set forth earlier: (1) you must know where you are on the ground and (2) you must know where you are going. Otherwise, as Yogi said, you may wind up somewhere else.

Down at Sea

Anyone who has done much extended overwater flying, say, to the far Out Islands of the Caribbean or from Florida or New Orleans to Cozumel or the Yucatan peninsula—or for that matter across Lake Erie or Lake Michigan or other inland seas—begins to consider sooner or later the possibility of going down on the water. The problem with "ditching" is that it is not a situation that can be simulated or practiced realistically by the average private pilot. It may be interesting to know that few military (i.e.: Air Force) pilots receive realistic ditching instruction, either; most of them are advised to depart the aircraft and descend by parachute because most of the smaller military aircraft tend to sink like a stone immediately after hitting the water. I remember the placard in a P-51 manual, suitably enclosed in a coffinlike frame, warning that after ditching the pilot had (as I remember) five seconds to get out, which ain't much when one is stunned by the sudden stop. Naval Aviators, who are required to qualify by landing and taking off from aircraft carriers under way at sea, are far more likely to need such training, therefore are introduced early in their cadet program (and renew their acquaintanceship regularly thereafter) with a device known to all aeronautical anchor clankers as "the Dilbert Dunker."

Simulation

The Dilbert Dunker is essentially a mockup of an aircraft cockpit, complete with simulated controls, configured as an actual cockpit would be on making either a catapult departure or an approach to an arrestment landing, that is: with the pilot strapped in, plugged in to oxygen and communications connections, wearing the full regalia prescribed by the safety regulations with the hatch fully open. The whole fazzafratz is mounted on an inclined track (the "glideslope") which descends to a huge tank of water, appropriately manned by a squad of scuba-equipped frogmen, the reason for whose presence soon becomes a matter of great personal interest to the student pilot.

The drill is for the student to strap and plug himself (and nowadays sometimes *her*self) into the rig, grasp the fake stick and throttle and brace for the splash, except when the dunker hits the water it turns upside down and begins to descend to the bottom, which is a looong way down. The occupant of the sinking rig is required to unplug, unsnap and unstrap him/herself while in the unusual and disoriented attitude and escape within ten or 15 seconds, otherwise the stand-by crew of scuba divers moves in, cuts all of the restraints, extracts the star of the piece and hauls him/her to the surface and the ministrations of the resuscitation squad.

It must be understood that before the actual escape experience under controlled conditions, the naval cadet has undergone a series of lectures and audio-visual experiences to prepare him for what he should expect, which few civilians have an opportunity to do. In addition, as part of his normal accouterments issued for flight duties a naval aviator (and naval aviator presumptive) has—and *wears* all the time while in flight regalia—an inflatable life vest and on his parachute pack is attached a one-man (person) inflatable dingy (for a fighter pilot); or, in the case of a larger airplane a multi-person inflatable life raft. The pilot has gone through dry-land drills or how to get the life saving equipment out of the aircraft after ditching, how to inflate it and get it into action with him on board. The speed with which a highly trained individual can perform under emergency conditions is remarkable and merits an illustrative story.

During the unpleasantness in the Pacific circa 1942 your deponent was the guest of the Nation on board a naval craft known as a destroyer, a misnomer at the time because of the nature of its assignment. The swift ship was one of a pair regularly stationed off the quarters of—Navy talk for "behind and on either side of"—an aircraft carrier when it was engaged in launching and/or taking aboard aircraft engaged in missions against the enemy. In actual practice the operations of an aircraft carrier rolling around on the open sea are not the routine Sunday-picnic that recruiting posters would have the public believe, especially when everyone in the operation is concerned about the possibility of an enemy submarine doing violence to the carrier made especially vulnerable because she has to forego the zig-zag aim-destroying pattern and hew a straight course into the wind to catapult airplanes off the bow and take them aboard over the stern (this was before the days of canted decks). The problem is amplified when any of the incoming aircraft are low on fuel or have sustained battle damage and, of course, the pilots are all emotionally and physically drained just when they need all of their flying skills. What happens is that from time to time an airplane doesn't make it. Sometimes a catapult-launched airplane would lose its engine just as it left the ship and splash, but more often an airplane coming in over the stern to land, with its gear down and full flaps extended, right on the edge of a stall would receive a wave-off from the Landing Signal Officer, possibly because the preceeding plane had fouled the arresting cables and blocked the landing area, and just as a light plane trying to go around with full flaps, the plane would slow down, rear up, the carrier outrun it and *splash*! An airplane and its crew was in the drink.

The function of the two trailing destroyers was to get over there and get the pilot out, pronto. (Now, helicopters are used for the same purpose.) It was a Dilbert Dunker drill, but for real, complete with a team of scuba divers perched on the destroyer's bow, ready to go over and get the crew out of the sinking plane. Without any publicity, those trailing "cans," as destroyers are referred to in naval circles, brought a lot of young pilots back from the deep.

Anyhow, on this particular day the big bird boat was aligned into the wind, aircraft were circling overhead forming up in trail to return to the coffee pot and the bridge of our ship was jammed with observers equipped with binoculars, telescopes (they call them "long glasses" in the Navy) and stationkeeping transits watching the returning planes returning to their floating nest when the reason for the assignment happened: a single engine fighter within what seemed to be touching distance of the deck suddenly flared off, dropped behind the carrier and plunged into the frothing wake, shooting up a geyser of spume 150 feet high. The destroyer heeled over under the helm, knifing through the sea at top speed towards the towering column marking the site of the crash as the frogmen slid their facemasks down and gripped their scuba mouthpieces with their teeth. It was a tense situation.

Then the gauzy curtain of spray settled and revealed the astonishing scene of a small figure wearing a helmet and goggles, kneeling in a fully inflated dinghy, paddling furiously toward us: the pilot. Except for the dampening effect of water falling back after the huge splash, he was dry—he didn't even get his feet wet! All he wanted from us when he came on board was a hot cup of java and a lift back to his ship.

While waiting for the equipment to be rigged to get him back into The Game, he was asked how in hell did he get out of the plane so fast? Most of the time, those life saving drills were troublesome, anxious experiences, not always successful. He grinned for a moment before he answered.

"Listen," he said, calmly lighting a cigarette. "For the last two years I have been instructing in ditching procedures and survival techniques at Corpus Christi, day in and day out. When that F6 quit flying, I reacted automatically without any conscious thought and went through all of the procedures that I had simulated so many times, zip-zip-zip."

"And", he added, as he rose to keep his date with the breeches buoy, "By God, it really works."

The message has never been forgotten here: prepare for the emergency, and practice, practice, practice.

A survey of water crashes and ditchings makes it clear that the majority of fatalities result from the failure of airmen either to have, or to be able to use—to launch, inflate and get into—life rafts and dinghies soon enough after the airplane is in the water. It is vitally important that one does not wait until the emergency happens to learn how to cope with it.

Going down on a broad expanse of water, whether it be one of the Great Lakes or a stretch of the Atlantic or Pacific Oceans or the blue Caribbean Sea, presents an entirely different set of survival problems from those we have discussed up to this point. However, since there is always a possibility of landing near—or on—a small island, the need for the basic land-oriented survival kit cannot be entirely discounted. Most of us think of survival gear in terms of flying to exotic new places: the Bahamas, or the Windward and Leeward Islands, or Baja California or in the Pacific Northwest, but many of us fly to resorts like Catalina Island, Marthas Vineyard, Nantucket or from Cleveland to Detroit or on over-water legs, as a matter of normal operation and as someone once said, the only difference between sea water and lake water is that you can drink the latter.

Floatation Gear

When preparing for vacation jaunts from Florida to the Bahamas or Islands of the Caribbean, we have each person in the airplane don a life vest (my wife calls them "pneumatic stoles") with dual means of inflation and make sure that each occupant knows how to inflate them, either by the CO_2 cartridge or by mouth. We also carry *in the cabin* an inflatable, Coast Guard-approved four-person inflatable life raft of bright yellow color, which packed in its container is about the size of a small suitcase ($7'' \times 11'' \times 25''$) and weighs 23 pounds. Such life rafts cost about $500 and Mae Wests cost about $75 each, so not everyone may want to invest that much in them. Since not everyone needs them frequently, arrangements can be made at many fixed base operators serving over-water flyers to rent them on a daily free basis. For example, virtually all of the FBOs in South Florida will rent floatation gear for island-hopping the Bahamas. However, let me say a few words about such gear.

Wear the Equipment!

I have lost count of the number of times I have seen groups of people heading out for the Bahamas from Florida with the rented life rafts and Mae Wests tossed casually into the luggage compartment. Believe me, if you hate to ditch, survival equipment so loaded will go down with the plane because it is impossible to open the luggage compartment door (except in Mooney aircraft) because of the pressure of the water against it. If floatation gear is to serve its purpose of saving you until the arrival of the Coast Guard, it must be immediately accessible without any difficulty, so that it can be pushed out of the door and inflated within seconds. It takes some forethought and at least a mental drill to get the equipment into action. Which brings me to another point. Many times I have observed island-bound airmen lay their life vests on the hat shelf. This is no good, either.

There is no way anyone—particularly if distraught, as by the feeling of an imminent dunking—can properly don a life vest within the confined cabin of a small airplane and get it on right, unless they have practiced several times. Mae West equipment is held in position by a series of straps so that it will support the head of an unconscious wearer and keep his face clear of the water and merely sorting out which strap attaches to which requires some bodily contortions, not easy to do in an airplane. The survival course instructors of the Navy at Jacksonville and Pensacola make it clear that having the equipment on and properly rigged will solve a great many problems if a ditching is required.

Briefing Time

Although it may go against your grain, since no one really likes to acknowledge the possibility of an accident to his airplane, there is absolutely no room for doubt that the odds for successful survival after a ditching are tremendously enhanced if everyone on board is thoroughly briefed on the proper procedures for, first, preparing for impact with the water; second, how to get out of the airplane *smartly* (a nautical term meaning "quickly," in a disciplined, rather than in a panicky manner) *with the life raft,* and third, how to launch it and inflate it. It can mean the difference between life and death if the occupants practice this operation several times, including the actual inflation (and deflation—and repacking) the life raft so that everyone will know what to do without being told or having to read a set of directions while treading water.

As mentioned before, we have seen people toss encased inflatable life saving vests into luggage compartments prior to heading out over the ocean to the Bahamas or islands in the Caribbean, but what is even more annoying is to see them put inflatable life rafts back there, too. The primary value of an inflatable vest is to keep you afloat while the raft is being inflated. Navy and Coast Guard Search and Rescue experts make it clear that an individual floating on the sparkling surface of the sea is one of the most difficult objects to spot; remember that only one's head and shoulders are exposed to view. On the other hand, a yellow raft or dinghy enlarges the object of the search so that the normal accommodation of the human eye can see it, whereas it may not be able to see the person floating upright. In the latter case a signalling mirror or orange smoke generator may be the ticket to survival when search aircraft appear in the vicinity. When venturing over water we each carry such signalling devices in waterproof containers on our persons, just in case.

The only place for an inflatable raft is *in the cabin,* positioned so that it can be launched immediately after impact. Our drill is to position the raft (which, in its container, is about the size of a large suitcase) so that immediately before impact the cabin door can be opened and the raft jammed into the gap to keep the door open after the splash. The raft itself is tied to the airplane with a 50′ length of light nylon line, secured in coils by rubber bands which will allow the line to extend freely. The reason for this is that when the CO_2 cartridges are activated to inflate the raft (which takes about 12 seconds), an unsecured raft is very likely to blow away in any kind of breeze, and once it is out of reach, no one in the water encumbered with clothing and an inflated life vest can catch up to it. So, we attach a tether to the raft, knotted every few feet so it won't slide through our hands, and we carry knives to slice through the attachment to the plane once the raft is transformed from a suitcase to a boat.

The Navy/Coast Guard recommended type of inflatable life raft has a complete cover to protect the occupants from the direct rays of the sun and from the glare off the water.

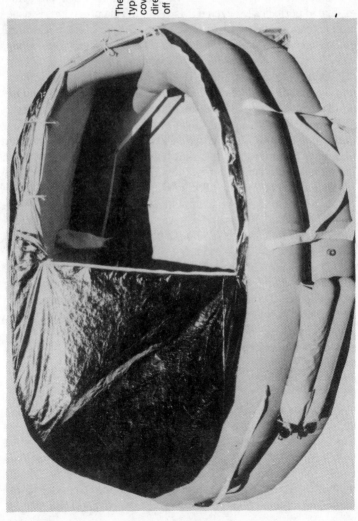

153

Never lose sight of the fact that the life raft is your *primary* survival device in ditching situations and that the inflatable life vest is a poor second according to the real experts, who should know.

Check Your Equipment!

Lightplane pilots who do not regularly (or, to put it another way, who seldom) fly over large expanses of water may make the economic determination that it is more practical to rent floatation gear for one of their sporadic island-hopping jaunts than to lay out several hundred dollars to buy their own. In any event, it is still recommended that the life saving equipment be inflated and examined periodically, even if it is rented. This procedure is especially recommended for personally-owned equipment because all unused rubberized fabric can deteriorate if kept in storage too long, whether it be in an airplane or the attic back home.

One of our closest friends over the years has been the internationally famous lightplane globetrotter, Marion Rice Hart, who has flown all over Europe, Africa, the Middle East, Asia, South America and North America in her single engine Beech Bonanza. In her peripatetic piloting, she has crossed the Mediterranian more often than the Phonecians and has shuttled up and down the Caribbean more than the Conquistadores. She has also flown her little airplane across the North Atlantic 18 times.

Some years ago, at the insistance of the Government of Canada, she equipped her Bonanza with certain equipment, including (as I recall) an ice axe, 50 feet of rope, a flashlight and a one-person life raft.

Recently at dinner the conversation turned to plans for the approaching winter, and after indicating that we were going to try for a couple of weeks on Harbour Island in the Bahamas, we inquired of Marion's plans, which are generally about as loose as a two minute egg. As usual the most we could get out of her was going to head south until it got warm, then stay there until winter went away back home.

"The Bahamas?" my wife inquired gently.

"No," sniffed la Hart. "I don't like local flights."

A few weeks later she told us that she believed that she would fly from Ft. Lauderdale direct to Puerto Rico (her "normal" fuel is nine hours, and with her long range tanks installed, 17 hours, so that wasn't any problem as far as she was concerned), then to Belize for a week or so, then across Mexico to Baja California, then back home to Washington, D.C. some time in May or June. Considering the extensive amount of water she would be overflying, I asked about her life raft, which she had said was still tucked away behind the cabin-mounted ferry tanks where she had put it several years before and where it had reposed over trips over seas and oceans I had never heard of, and countries only recently invented. Not until after considerable conversation on my part did she agree to have the thing taken out and inspected, which she did at Red Aircraft on Ft. Lauderdale airport.

You guessed it. The fabric had cracked and rotted and deteriorated so badly that they couldn't inflate it with a high pressure air hose. The "life" raft had more holes in it than a political platform and was totally worthless for anything except creating black smoke if thrown on a roaring fire. It does not make sense to carry a piece of equipment that seemingly complies with the rules for overwater flying, if it is really useless for saving your life.

Realistic Practice

Survival experts also recommend that pilots who have floatation equipment take it to a swimming pool and practice inflating it, both by the primary method (CO_2 cylinders) and back-ups (inflation by lung power), then practice getting into it and out of it and righting it from an upside down position. We regularly use our own four-man liferaft for skin diving in the Bahamas where the surface can sometimes become quite rough when there is a good breeze, and have learned some of the problems involved, not the least of which was having the doggoned thing blow away despite the trailing line stretched out behind it in the water. Now, we also rig a drogue or "sea anchor" so that if we ever *do* fall out in a heavy sea, the raft won't sail off. Practicing in the water will also teach the necessity of securing everything—emergency transmitter locator, smoke generators, flare guns, strobe lights, signalling mirrors, fresh water canteens, knives and *occupants*—to the raft itself.

The survival course presented by Aircraft Owners and Pilots Association (AOPA) has included in its syllabus of post-crash survival techniques actual in-the-water floatation equipment drills in addition to the use of the survival kit and survival-on-land part of the course, mentioned earlier in this book. I highly recommend that anyone who flies should sign up for the AOPA course the next time it is available in his/her area.

Ditching Procedures

The technique of ditching an airplane is too complicated to cover fully in a chapter, or an entire book, for so much depends on the type of airplane and its individual characteristics: high wing vs. low wing, fixed gear vs. retractable, engine location and cooling systems. I must say that after my experience at the Navy's survival school at Jacksonville, if I had my druthers for a ditchable airplane it would be a single engine, low wing retractable. However, I remember the warning (enclosed in that coffin-like design) in my P-51 manual to the effect that, even in the event of a successful ditching, the aircraft would sink within five seconds!

As with any off-airport landing, the pilot should approach the point of touch-down at the slowest possible *controllable* airspeed, with the least amount of sink-rate, having first made sure that every occupant is strapped in tight and that there is no loose baggage adrift in the cabin—especially on the hat shelf. If possible, one should land parallel to the wave forms, rather than directly into the face (even the rear face) of a wave. Water is incompressible hence is as hard as concrete on impact, so that hitting a large swell head-on is akin to flying into a bridge abutment and is something to be avoided. Landing a low wing plane, gear up, on a smooth, glancing contact often creates a smooth deceleration and a relatively easy exit. Furthermore, especially if its tanks are empty, a low wing plane will tend to float upright for quite a while, sometimes up to 15 or 20 minutes. I know of two cases where people, trying to stretch their fuel inbound from the Bahamas, landed in the Gulf Stream and were picked up, literally without getting their hair wet.

High wing airplanes, and low wingers with fixed gear, present other problems in ditching attempts. Although most fixed gears will be bent all awry upon contacting the water (about the way they would be bent by hitting the "lip" of a runway end, as in the case of a short landing), the result is frequently an upsetting or overturning of the airplane and you must be prepared for such an eventuality. This is why the Navy uses the mockup in which they dump cadets into a tank of water, slowly turning the whole simulator upside down so that the student will learn how to get out when everything is very confusing. Interestingly enough, where a high wing retractable may sink to the level of the wings if it stays upright, one that flips on its back will frequently float and be easy to exit, since the doors are above the water—and water pressure. In any event, keep in mind the problems of (a) landing under control and (b) getting the hell out of the airplane *with* floatation gear.

Call For Help Right Away

Over many routes the FAA maintains flight-following services, such as across the Great Lakes and to offshore islands; in addition, the FAA maintains oceanic air traffic control facilities and constant communication with the air traffic control systems of other countries: the Bahamas, Canada, Mexico and Cuba. Therefore, anyone flying in the Bahamas, Caribbean area, in the Gulf of Mexico, or offshore by as much as 100 miles, can communicate emergency messages on the oceanic control frequencies to the private network of commercial aeronautical radio stations (Airinc), or to the aircraft they are talking to and advise of a developing problem. Any radio transmission that begins "Pan-pan-pan..." will get priority and if you have to holler "Mayday" you will get everyone's immediate, undivided attention. Any pilot who proposes to fly in any oceanic control area should consult with the FAA or check his instrument (radio facility) charts, both for the low route and high route (jet) structures and note the radio frequencies for the areas involved. Generally speaking, the higher you fly, the longer your VHF radio signal will reach, although it is amazing how far away air carriers to 35,000 feet and up can hear you and forward your message. The main thing in any search and rescue situation is to notify someone immediately if you have—or think you may have—any problem aloft, giving your position and intentions. If you do have to do down, *someone* will come looking for you.

After the Splash

Once out of the plane, which will surely sink after a while unless the wings have been filled with pingpong balls, it is important to inflate the life raft (it takes about ten seconds), then get all of the plane's occupants into it and prepare to wait for rescue. Survival at sea has an entirely different set of problems than those on land.

First of all, particularly in the semi-tropical and tropical regions, it is vitally important to keep all skin areas covered to protect against sunburn, which can be incapacitating and in extreme cases, deadly. Under the direct rays of the sun, particularly if the skin is wet, the epithelial surface is affected about as if someone had taken a swipe at it with a blowtorch, or it was seared in a gasoline flash fire, which is to say, second degree burns. It is bad enough to have a raw nose, cheeks, ears, lips, neck and hands, any of which can be extremely painful and incapacitating, but a serious over-all exposure can result in a number of physical problems with grave complications, up to kidney failure and uremic poisoning, even death. These situations are particularly complicated because of the shortage of drinking water after a few days.

However, there is relatively little physical activity for anyone who is confined to a small life raft so that the principle of water conservation by reducing transpiration losses will tend to prevent any severe upset in the water balance of the body.

Exposure Problems at Sea

Exposure to continuous dampness, the chilling effect of the almost ever-present wind and the unrelieved glare of the sun creates serious physical problems for anyone adrift at sea in a small liferaft, even in the warm waters of the tropics and semi-tropics. Over many years of practical experience, the U.S. Navy has learned that the anticipation of a calamity leads to preparing to meet the exigency and as a result has created many naval air operations rules. One of these has to do with air crews wearing appropriate clothing in accordance with the mission assigned, and although at first glance some of the rules seem arbitrary (if not nutty) anyone who regularly reads the Navy air safety publication *Approach* will see that the requirements are sound and that non-compliance frequently results in unnecessary personal injury.

For example, naval airmen are required to wear headgear known variously as "crash helmets", "hard hats" or "brain buckets" when flying, even if flying civilian type off-the-shelf lightplanes used for training or liaison functions. It may seem silly to civilians who fly exactly the same kind of airplanes wearing no more than a baseball cap, but after reading about violent landings where the pilot's head ricochetted off assorted hard and unyielding parts of the aircraft structure, or worse, where a pilot was stunned by banging his head against a canopy or the overhead in heavy turbulence, which could have disastrous results, all of which could have been avoided by wearing the hard hats.

Following their lead, I hied over to the local sporting goods store and bought a baseball batting helmet made of stout plastic and well padded, which I put under the seat of the Cherokee Six. The very next flight we made passed through a heavy rainstorm and cloud buildup, so I donned the batting helmet, just in time: a violent bounce rapped my head against the windowsill hard enough to loosen my fillings. I really believe that if I had not been wearing that protection on my sconce that I could have been another of those unexplained NTSB statistics.

However, the theme here is that the Navy tells its pilots that if they ever have to ditch and wait for search and rescue for a day or so while bobbing around in their life rafts, they must not take off or throw away their heavy crash helmets but should wear them for protection against the burning rays of the sun and furthermore they should protect their eyes against glare by lowering a tinted visor or wearing sunglasses. The moral: be sure that you have head protection against the blazing sun if you are in a survival at sea situation. A broad brimmed hat is some protection but a French Foreign Legion

ANY HAT CAN BE RIGGED TO PUT YOU IN THE FOREIGN LEGION

DOWN AT SEA: ALL YOU CAN DO IS WAIT

Down at sea; all you can do is wait.

rig, covering your neck, face and ears from both the direct and indirect (i.e.: reflected) rays of the sun is better. Keep the sun from burning your skin.

Another garment required by the Navy is an anti-exposure coverall known colloquially in the trade as the "poopie suit". At one time I was of the opinion that the poopie suit was designed to preserve airmen downed in frigid water such as is found in the North Atlantic or Pacific Oceans, Antarctica, for the lethal aspects of being immersed in ice cold water are horrifying—immersion in water at the freezing level will result in unconsciousness within minutes and death soon afterwards. But in *Approach* I read that airmen downed in warm seas should retain and continue to wear their antiexposure coveralls, their hard hats, their shoes and socks and the regular-issue lightweight flight gloves designed to prevent burns from flash

OLD FASHIONED SLICKERS OR
SOU'WESTERS ARE THE BEST
PROTECTION AT SEA

A BASEBALL CAP, RIGGED WITH
A HANDKERCHIEF TO MAKE A
BEAU GESTE HEAD COVERING IS
REQUIRED FOR BRIGHT SUN EXPOSURE
SITUATIONS. ALWAYS WEAR EYE
PROTECTION!

Protection from the sun, including protection for your eyes, is a primary concern if down at sea.

fires in crash situations. The dual threats to airmen down at sea against which wearing such protective gear is important, according to *Approach* are sunburn and dehydration due both to the sun and the constant breeze which blows over the ocean surface. Wearing the protective clothing practically eliminates dehydration due to evaporation of perspiration (which incidentally is why motorcycle buffs and pilots of open framework aircraft like "Breezies" should wear leather jackets and trousers). After discussions with acknowledged experts on overcoming the problems of survival on the open ocean, we follow all of the advice they give particularly when, again and again we hear those marine rescue experts advise that anyone who is going to have to spend more than an hour or two afloat in a small completely open boat or raft on the ocean, especially in the tropics or semi-tropics, should at the very minimum wear a long sleeved shirt, long trousers, a sun-visored or wide brimmed hat, plus gloves, socks and back-of-the-neck and face protection from the direct and reflected rays of the sun. The warning is that any skin exposed to those rays can be literally cooked.

As a result, our practice is to wear long sleeved shirts (usually with the sleeves rolled up) and long pants whenever overflying wide expanses of water and we also tuck a pair of cotton stockings and a pair of light cotton gloves into the hip pockets and a couple of tubes of sun-blocking ointment in our shirt pockets. It is also wise to carry a couple of large pocket handkerchiefs. One of them can be used to make a Foreign Legion-type sunburn protector for the back of your neck.

We also fasten a large tightly wrapped sheet to our life raft, to be used as an over-all sunshade, sort of a tentlike affair patterned after the Navy (and Air Force) design of emergency life rafts.

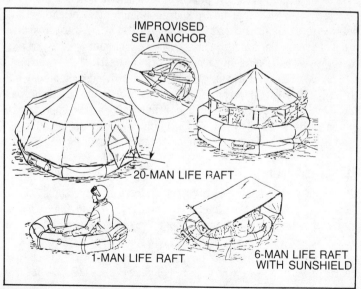

IMPROVISED SEA ANCHOR

20-MAN LIFE RAFT

1-MAN LIFE RAFT

6-MAN LIFE RAFT WITH SUNSHIELD

Other types of life rafts.

And Then, There's Seasickness

No matter how smooth the surface of the sea may look from a mile above, there will always be some wave action which will affect the raft in which you are cradled. It may not be rough and choppy, although it *can* become bad enough to overturn a raft—which requires that all hands on board be secured to the raft by lengths of nylon line.

No matter that a long swell system may seem like swinging in a hammock for an hour or so, unless you are a seaman who is used to the motion (which never stops) you may become seasick, a condition which has been described as "At first, you think you are going to die; then you become afraid that you *aren't* going to die". Motion-induced nausea as a result of a small craft's bobbing like a cork on the surface of a rolling sea is not only highly disagreeable, it can lead to dehydration, about which we have spoken before. So, it is wise to have a bottle of anti-seasick pills in your floatation equipment. Obviously taking pills requires that you have drinking water available and this brings us back to the U.S. Army type of web belt equipment: canteens cum canteen cups which can be kept together in a handy location in the cabin for immediate retrieval in the event of a descent to the water. Most military surplus stores sell such belts, canteens (be sure the canteen cups are included), and an assortment of containers that will attach to the belt with special hooks, including first aid pouches, cartridge pouches, special equipment containers (our favorite is an 81mm mortar sight-container made of leather) and automatic weapons' magazine-containers. Some of these pouches are just about right for carrying signalling equipment—flares, smoke markers, dye markers, signalling mirrors and shark (ugh!) repellent. If possible, we would also like to take our basic fishing equipment and the AR-7 survival rifle, which could supply us with food if rescue was for some reason delayed. Raw fish or meat may not be appealing to anyone who is used to poached salmon or duck l'orange, but remember the old adage that hunger is the best cook.

All You Can Do Is Wait

Once you have settled everyone in the rubberized boat, about all you can do is wait for someone to come pick you up. There is not much hope for sailing such a craft, but if you have planned for survival and have triggered S&R, and have your signalling devices ready, rescue is usually a matter of hours.   Remember, with a couple of quarts of water anyone who does not engage in physical activities can last a long time.

For crash-landing situations a baseball batting helmet quickly available from beneath your seat is a worthwhile addition to one's flying gear.

Special Signalling Devices

Although we will get into signalling in somewhat more detail in the next chapter, a word must be said here about two devices which are especially valuable in down-at-sea situations.

Earlier, we said that the odds are against anyone searching for a downed aircraft at night. This may be true for land-type searches, but is *not* true for water search and rescue activities when it is very important to reach the dunked survivors as quickly as possible. Search aircraft with radar altimeters can fly over water without any fear of encountering high terrain, such as mountains or microwave towers, hence will, and do make air sweeps in the dead of night. To make your location clear the first device is an emergency locator beacon, preferably the type that will float and if possible, with voice transmission capability. An ELT will bring the search planes directly to your position and we have a number of instances in which *yachts* equipped with emergency radio beacons have been located and their crews saved within hours after their devices were activated. Most of the successful search and rescue operations took place three hundred miles *or more* from shore-based rescue planes of the U.S. Coast Guard. Some manufacturers of marine (i.e.: for yachts) ELT equipment already produce watertight, floatable ELTs. We have two, sometimes three ELTs in our Cherokee Six: a quick-detach installation SHARC-7 which has its own microphone, plus small personnel-type units which we carry on our persons; for overwater trips they are placed in water-proof plastic bags.

The other night-time device is a hand-held waterproof, flashlight battery-powered strobe light which flashes a brilliant white light about once every second and will last for several hours with fresh batteries. For overwater hops, these strobe lights are must items, because even on the darkest of nights the bright pinpoint of light can be seen for miles from a search plane.

When speaking over the ELT transmitter, hold the antenna vertically for best reception in all directions.

Water Markers

Another excellent locator for finding people on (or in) the water is the Navy-developed dye marker. Tossing the contents of a dye marker on the surface of the ocean creates a large smear of unnatural color which spreads over the surface to make a quickly recognizable area from the air. We usually have a couple of dye markers in our survival kits, really as a back-up system. They don't take up much room, don't weigh much and, as the saying goes, every little bit helps.

Initiating Rescue Operations

The First Step—Set Up An "Overdue" Alert

The First Step to Rescue is the one that costs the least. All it takes is a telephone call to let someone at the far end of your flight know that you are (a) going to make the trip, (b) what your route will be, (c) when you plan to take off, and (d) how long the trip will take, so that your estimated time of arrival (ETA) will be understood by someone who can alert official search and rescue (SAR) officials. If no one knows you are flying, or overdue, no one will even begin to come looking, at least for several days —if then.

Flight Plans

In normal operations, the easiest way to set up a notification program is simply to file a Visual Flight Plan with your local FAA Flight Service Station. This, of course, is not required for flight under visual conditions—a point that non-aviators cannot seem to get through their heads, as if having (or not having) a "flight plan" makes any difference in the actual operation of aircraft. There has been some effort by U.S. Government budgeteers to eliminate Visual Flight Plans, which in my opinion reflects a callous disregard for the public safety, for the Flight Service/Civil Air Patrol relationship has been responsible for thousands of successful rescue operations.

FEDERAL AVIATION AGENCY FLIGHT PLAN					FROM APPROVED BUDGET BUREAU NO. 04-R072 3			
		I. TYPE OF FLIGHT PLAN		2. AIRCRAFT IDENTIFICATION				
		FVFR		VFR	X	NIMV		
		IFR		DVFR				
3. AIRCRAFT TYPE/SPECIAL EQUIPMENT PA32/A	4. TRUE AIRSPEED 135 KNOTS	5. POINT OF DEPARTURE ABQ	6 DEPARTURE TIME		7. INITIAL CRUISING ALTITUDE 8000			
			PROPOSED(Z) 1600	ACTUAL (Z)				
8. ROUTE OF FLIGHT V12 PRESCOTT VIO5								
9. DESTINATION (NAME OF AIRPORT AND CITY) LAS VEGAS MCCARREN	10. REMARKS NOTIFY HUGHES NEVADA DIVISION IF SUSPECTED OVERDUE 702-739-1100							
11. ESTIMATED TIME/ROUTE		12. FUEL ON BOARD		13. ALTERNATE AIRPORT(S)		14. PILOT'S NAME		
HOURS	MINUTES	HOURS	MINUTES	NONE		F.K. SMITH		
3	10	5	45					
15. PILOT'S ADDRESS & TELEPHONE NO. OR AIRCRAFT HOME BASE DCA/PAGE AIRWAYS	16. NO. OF PERSONS ABOARD 2	17. COLOR OF AIRCRAFT WHITE ORANGE & TAN TRIM	18. FLIGHT WATCH STATIONS ZUNI- WINSLOW- PRESCOTT- PEACH SPRINGS					
CLOSE FLIGHT PLAN UPON ARRIVAL			SPECIAL EQUIPMENT SUFFIX A — DME & 4096 CODE TRANSPONDER A — DME & 64 CODE TRANSPONDER D — DME	L — DME & TRANSPONDER —NO CODE T — 64 CODE TRANSPONDER U — 4096 CODE TRANSPONDER X — TRANSPONDER - NC CODE					

FAA FORM   7233-I   (4.66) FORMERLY FAA 398   0052-027-8000

File a Flight Plan; the first step of a search and rescue operation.

Personal Telephone Calls

However, although you file a Visual Flight Plan, I also recommend that you call someone at your intended point of destination to have two strings to your bow. Unfortunately, if you depend entirely on a Visual Flight Plan, it may take a day or so to slip the SAR mission into gear, simply because so many thoughtless, forgetful or stupid pilots complete flights without closing their flight plans with the FAA that when an airplane shows up as overdue, Flight Service Specialists routinely go through the first step of calling all the airports and fixed base operators in their vicinity to see if the so-called "missing" airplane is actually down or has actually landed without notifying them. Sometimes, it may take as long as 24 to 48 hours before the Civil Air Patrol is alerted and on the move, which means that a downed airman must spend an equivalently longer time in the wilds. That is why it seems advisable to have a back-up alerting system so that the Flight Service folks will *know* that your airplane is indeed overdue. Of course, if the weather conditions are too bad for visual flying, required for search operations, the effort will not begin anyhow, until it improves enough to be able to see a downed aircraft.

Better still, of course, are radio communications with ground stations and other aircraft. When aviating in the best of weather, we call in to just about all of the Flight Service Stations (Airways Radio) along the route, so that our aircraft number will be logged. Then, if we become overdue, the along-the-route stations can be queried and the probable position of the forced landing be narrowed down, which will make the SAR effort more efficient. In addition, we are at all times prepared to advise someone by radio of a developing predicament, either Flight Service, another aircraft, or an Air Route Traffic Control Center (ARTCC, usually referred to simply as "Center"). On our flight plan form we note the Center frequencies as shown on our Jeppesen Navigation charts, so that we can alert them, or another airplane on the frequency, if we have any—or *think* we have any—problem in flight. I remember one flight in our old Apache in beautiful sunny weather, from Greensboro to Knoxville. Right over the jagged mountains of Tennessee both engines began to run very rough and, when I pulled on full carburetor heat, quit. Both of them, at the same time, simultaneously and together, quit cold. I immediately called Atlanta Center and asked them to hold my hand until I got everything together. Fortunately, the judicious application of a little carb heat at a time cleaned out the ice in the carburetors and I was able to relax again—about two days later, that is. Taught me a lesson, though: you can pick up carb ice in severe-clear weather.

The Pay-off

No matter what, it is really helpful mentally in any situation of stress to have a realistic basis for *hope*, or to put it another way, that the situation in which you have been plunged is not hopeless. If you know that (a) someone responsible will know that you have not completed the trip as planned, that (b) an overdue report will be followed up by the FAA and the word passed to the Civil Air Patrol, the airlines, the Air Force, Navy and Coast Guard, and (c) that you have the equipment and the ability to use it that will enable you to hold out and be in good shape until they come and snatch you out of the wilderness, you will be mentally and psychologically adjusted to survive the ordeal, great or minor as it may be.

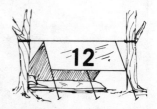

How Are They Going to Find You?

Once someone knows that you are down, a search will be initiated by the Civil Air Patrol, the Air Force, the Navy, the Coast Guard—or in Canada, the Royal Canadian Air Force and in the Bahamas, by the great volunteer group known as Bahamas Air Sea Rescue Association (BASRA)—usually with the help of airline pilots who are flying over the area and can receive your ELT distress signal. Once the search teams know approximately where you are, they will concentrate on combing that area by eyes from aloft. Therefore, your job is to make yourself as conspicuous as possible so that they will see you.

We have already alluded to the issue of being located in a down-at-sea situation; here we will be discussing only the problems of being found on dry land.

The First Line

Again, the greatest aid is the emergency locator transmitter—if it works. They do not always work, either because their batteries have run down—as in the case of turning them on too soon so that the batteries simply poop out before the signal can be heard by anyone—or because airframe vibration has caused screws to loosen in the innards of the aircraft-mounted ETL. It is worthwhile to have the, pardon the expression, "guts" of your ELT checked periodically by someone who knows about it.

As you know, we have two—sometimes three—ELTs in the Wander Bird: one mounted to the airframe by velcro pads plus a quickly detachable metal strap (with its own microphone) plus one

The Narco Marine EPIRB (Emergency Position Indicating Radio Beacon), which is a sea-borne ELT and transmits, just like aviation ELT's (Emergency Locator Transmitters) on 121.5 and 243.0 MHz, the civil and military distress frequencies. It is waterproof, floats, and measures 4″ × 8¾″ × 4½″.

each for my wife and me. In airmens' parlance, this is known as triple-redundency. The ELT is the first line of location equipment, for all S&R aircraft have VHF homing devices that will follow the signal, whether it is from the middle of a dense forest, buried under a snowbank or covered with blowing sand.

The Second Line

The *second line* of location equipment is the simplest, cheapest and yet one of the most effective—as long as the sun is out and in the right position. It is the basic Air Force/Navy signalling mirror.

The signalling mirror does not have to be large; ours are made of shockproof plastic, silvered on both sides, fit into a normal, sized shirt pocket and cost about three or four dollars. The signalling mirror is designed with a hole in its center through which you can sight with great precision directly at an object. Believe me, when the sun is out, the blindingly bright flash from the mirror can be seen for

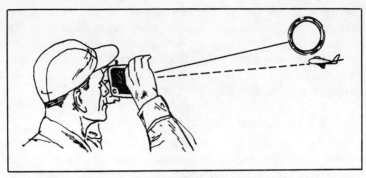

Using the signalling mirror: 1) Hold the mirror a few inches in front of your face; a small spot of sunlight will come through the center hole and fall on your face. 2) Sight the search plane through the hole in the mirror. 3) By adjusting the angles of the mirror so that the sun-spot on your face disappears through the hole while you are sighting the aircraft through the same hole, you will reflect the sun's rays directly at the aircraft. 4) Once certain that the airman has seen you, stop any further flashing because it is blindingly bright.

tremendous distances. Last summer when I was flying from Washington, D.C. to our home in Ocean City, N.J., one of my sons who was waiting for me at the Ocean City Intentional Airpatch began to scan the horizon towards the west, in the direction from which I was arriving. From 3,000 feet over the Delaware Bay I could *see* that flashing light, even though, being some 30 miles away, he could not

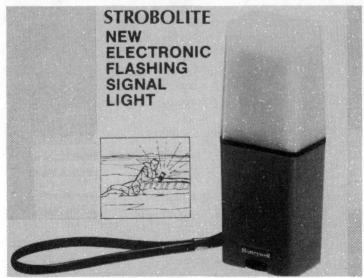

The Honeywell strobolite is a must item for over-water flying. Waterproof, it produces a high-intensity flash, 300 times brighter than an ordinary flashlight, up to seven hours per set of "C" batteries.

171

see my airplane! That intermittent pinpoint of light, against the general background of reflections of afternoon sunlight from the waters of Ocean City's bayside, and the windshields of boats and cars, was unmistakable as a signal and completely convinced me that a signalling mirror must always be in my pocket when flying across wild country. And so will my co-pilot carry one, too.

Possible Radio Communications

If the airplane's electrical system and its radios, including antennas, have come through the experience unscathed, you may be able to direct search and (especially!) rescue operations from your ground-based control center, which is a tremendous help to the people above who can act better on the detailed information you can supply them concerning the status of the ones on the ground and food supplies, etc.

If you have an emergency locator transmitter with a voice circuit built in, you can (if you have a microphone) speak to search and rescue aircraft on the distress frequency (121.5 MHz) and if you also have a small battery powered portable VHF receiver as so many pilots tote along to check aviation weather, you can listen to them on that. Two-way voice communications have it all over signalling panels and body signals.

Close-in Visual Signals

We discussed making signal fires a while back, including how one can make white smoke by throwing damp leaves and pine needles on the blaze, or make black smoke by burning oil and rubber. Both will work, if the wind is calm, so that a tower of smoke can be seen. But if it is very windy, smoke from a signal fire is whisked away and hard to spot against a background of trees or other wilderness, such as the Great Southwestern Desert. The best smoke signal is created chemically, and produces either a billowing red or orange cloud, neither of which can be mistaken for a product of nature, as smoke from a wood-based signal fire might be.

A couple of years ago, a lightplane went down in Western Canada and for more than a week no one in the S&R team could find it. Then one day a passenger in an Air Canada jet flying at 33,000 feet happened to look down and saw a swath of orange smoke laying across the miles of greenery below, alerted a stewardess who in turn alerted the captain. Within a few minutes help was on the way to the pinpointed location and the pilot was saved. Except in a gale force wind, the orange smoke will make a clearly distinguishable distress signal against any background and in a ten mile an hour wind will lay a

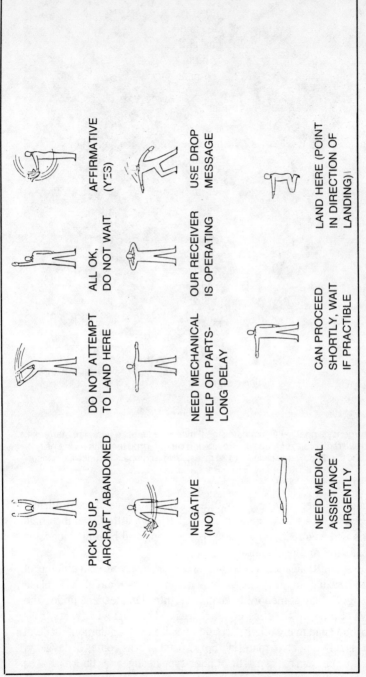

Body signals for communication with search aircraft.

173

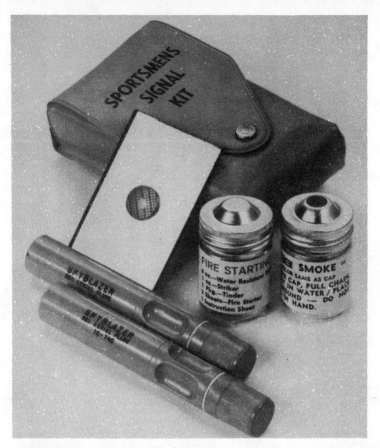

Emergency signal kit: Contains a signal mirror, red smoke flare, fire starter kit, and two red skyblazer flares that reach an altitude of 400 feet with an intensity of 20,000 candlepower, visible up to 20 miles. All in a compact 5-ounce kit measuring 5″ × 3″ × 2″. Courtesy Eddie Bauer, Inc.

cloud 100 feet wide and 1,500 feet long. We have at least a half a dozen orange smoke generators in their own little three inch high cans and frequently give them to our flying and boating friends as small gifts and remembrances.

Along that line, we recommend that everyone have some of that amazing material known by various names (″dayglow″; ″blaze orange″) that somehow becomes brightly luminescent under the rays of the sun. Sporting goods stores sell hats, gloves, vests, rolls of ribbon and many other garments and items of equipment made of this highly reflective material. Spray paint in cans comes in dayglow, also, so you can make plastic or fiber-type headgear as fluorescent as

Ground-to-air emergency code using panels, stones, brush, or stamped-out in snow. Symbols should be 12 × 18 feet in size.

1. REQUIRE DOCTOR—SERIOUS INJURIES.	2. REQUIRE MEDICAL SUPPLIES.	3. UNABLE TO PROCEED.	4. REQUIRE FOOD AND WATER.	5. REQUIRE FIREARMS AND AMMUNITION.	6. INDICATE DIRECTION TO PROCEED.
7. AM PROCEEDING IN THIS DIRECTION.	8. WILL ATTEMPT TO TAKE OFF.	9. AIRCRAFT BADLY DAMAGED.	10. PROBABLY SAFE TO LAND HERE.	11. ALL WELL.	12. REQUIRE FUEL AND OIL.
13. NO-NEGATIVE.	14. YES-AFFIRMATIVE.	15. NOT UNDERSTOOD.	16. REQUIRE MECHANIC.	17. REQUIRE COMPASS AND MAP.	18. REQUIRE SIGNAL EQUIPMENT.

LETTER "STROKE SIZE" IN RATIO OF 1 TO 6.
(3 FEET WIDE × 18 FEET HIGH STROKES)
LETTER WIDTH SIZE IN APPROXIMATE RATIO 2 TO 3.
(12 WIDE × 18 FEET HIGH)

175

the hunters' hats. We also have two sets of dayglow rain gear (jackets and pants), usually used for untying (or tying down) the airplane on rainy days and performing the pre-flight routine. They certainly make one highly visible.

Sporty's in Cincinnati supplied us with some day-glow signalling panels, originally in 4' × 9' size, which we have re-cut to 2' × 9' for our own use. Eight panels fold to about the size of a wool shirt for storage and weigh less than a pound.

Pyrotechnics, etc.

Some stores do a brisk business in various types of flares, flare guns and rockets. My own feeling is that, except for water rescue operations at night such items are not always very useful. As mentioned before, most air-searches will be conducted during the hours of daylight in reasonably good weather, not during the dark of night or in conditions of reduced visibility. However, highway-type flares (the kind police use to warn of road hazards) will burn brightly, hotly and for a long time and we have some in the airplane's survival kit to use as a back-up emergency fire starter. With one of those lighted at

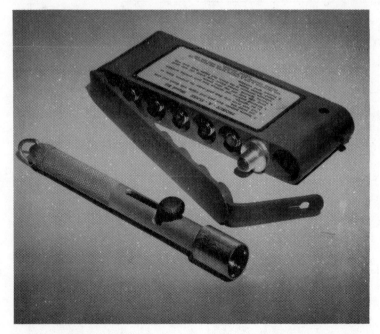

The Project-A-Flare Signal Kit is an extremely valuable signalling device, but since it uses powder to project the flare it is sold only by licensed gun dealers.

the middle of a prepared pile of wood, ignition is almost guaranteed. We used to carry a flare pistol with a full set of flare cartridges, but have concluded that the combination of a strong ELT signal and a close-in locator signal, orange smoke, dayglow panels and dress, signalling mirrors and, at night, bright strobe lights, will do the job.

On the same theory as the orange smoke generator— remember the airline passenger who saw the smoke and alerted the captain?—we take our strobes along on all flights. Who knows? Maybe a passenger on a night flight might alert the stewardess.......

I must add that the same comment applies to the dye marker packets when flying to the Bahamas, the Caribbean islands or to the eastern coast of Mexico from Florida or the Keys.

Happy Ending

It is human nature to put aside all negative thoughts and hope that life will always proceed on an even keel, but let's face it, accidents do happen. That is why we buy all sorts of insurance coverages on our homes, on our cars, on our airplanes and on ourselves. Insurance, simply means "protection against loss" and can take many other forms than an agreement written on a piece of legal paper. Insurance can be as basic as holding on to a bannister rail while descending the stairs—which is incidentally the most danger-ous thing most of us do every day, yet take for granted. Have you ever considered the consequences of pitching from the top of a staircase? Or, it can be (for pilots) taking regular recurrent multi-engine or instrument flight instruction—or preparing for the worst emergency that one can imagine. The object is to continue to live after or in spite of an incident or accident—which may in fact never happen. Remember that old Western adage to the effect that a man might carry a gun for years and years and never need it, but when he *does* need it, he needs it damn bad and the biggest gun is none too big. And think on it.

The same philosophy applies to survival kits. For years our family—our three sons are all pilots and Marianne is my regular copilot—has flown all over Canada, Mexico, the Bahamas and the Caribbean, and to all of the "Southern Forty-eight" States, without incident or any actual need for the somewhat bulky and admittedly heavy (the whole package, the grab-bag, the Big Red Bag and five gallons of fresh water weighs in at 100 pounds for winter survival) but a few weeks ago, when we bucked the winter weather from Washington, D.C. to Las Vegas to attend an aviation convention, weather changed our routing from D.C. almost direct to Oklahoma City, Albuquerque, Winslow and on to Las Vegas to an unpredictable routing via Pittsburgh, Peoria, Kansas City and Amarillo before we got on our planned route, and we got a good look at all kinds of weather; snow, extreme cold, freezing rain and gusty headwinds, which put us on the ground several times at least for an overnight stay. Then, our routing home was even more circuitous: from Las Vegas we flew over Phoenix to Tucson, Arizona (where the runway had just been cleared of six inches of snow!) then continued south to Cabo Sun Lucas, at the very southern tip of Baja California. Then we flew directly to Matamoros, over the Sierra Madre Mountains, thence to New Orleans, Atlanta and home. On that one trip we had experienced just about every climatic variation one can have, from sub-zero cold to semi-tropic heat and most of the time we were traversing wild, uninhabited and sometimes desolate country. But no matter where we might have gone down, we knew that that extra weight on the floor behind our seats would give us the ability to survive until help arrived, even if it took a week.

We love to fly and to go to new places that we used to read about only in the pages of the *National Geographic*. But we no longer sail off to the Caribbean with only Bermuda shorts, lightweight shirts and a couple of suitcases. And whenever I read of anyone flying in the Arctic in a single engine airplane's "shirtsleeve environment," it makes me shudder. Only a couple of years ago I lost a good friend and his son who made a successful precautionary landing in Idaho, because of a blizzard which closed down the mountain passes, and froze to death. If only...

They are the words we hear again and again after a serious or fatal accident. "If only..." What we have tried to do is prepare on the basis of two better words: "What if?" Then, if the worst ever *does* happen, we will be able to tell about it some day to our grandchildren. And our story will have a happy ending.

Appendices

Appendix
Recommended Reading:

Special Study on Emergency Landing Techniques in Small Fixed Wing Aircraft
Report No. NTSB-AAS-72-3
Available from National Transportation Safety Board
            Washington, D.C. 20591

Four books by Bradford Angier:
   How to Stay Alive in the Woods; Colier Pubs
   On Your Own in the Wilderness; Stackpole
   Living Off the Country; Stackpole
   Home in Your Pack (especially, "A Modern Outdoorsman's First Aid Kit Pack") Colier pubs.

Two Books by Dian Thomas (Warner Books):
   Roughing it Easy
   Roughing it Easy 2

Three Books by Ewell Gibbons (David McKay Co.)
      Stalking the Wild Asparagus;
      Stalking the Blue Eyed Scallop;
      Stalking the Healthful Herbs

Anyone Can Live Off the Land, J.R. Johnson (David McKay Co.)

Edible Wild Plants, Oliver P. Medsger (MacMillan Co.)

A Pilot's Survival Manual, Nesbit, Pond, Allen

Plane Safety and Survival, Anderson, Aero Publishers

And, if you are a member of Aircraft Owners and Pilots Association, by all means take the *AOPA Survival Course* whenever it is scheduled in your area.

The Official Boy Scout Fieldbook)
    Workman Publishing Co., N.Y.
    1 West 39th St., N.Y. City 10018)
Colorado "Outward Bound"
    945 Pennsylvania Avenue
    Denver, Colorado 80203

And the "BIBLE": Air Force Manual AFM 64-6
                  Search and Rescue SURVIVAL
                  dated 15 August 1969
                  Department of the Air Force
                  For Sale by the Superintendent of Documents
                  U.S. Government Printing Office Washington,
                  D.C. 20402 Price $1.50

And the Canadian "BIBLE": *Down but not Out* (Royal Canadian Air
                        Force)
                        Canadian Government Printing
                        Centre
                        Supply and Services Canada
                        Hull, Quebec, Canada K1A 0S9
                        Price: $6.50

Standard First Aid to Personal Safety $1.95
Advanced First Aid & Emergency Aid $2.30
    Doubleday & Co. Inc.
    501 Franklin Ave.
    Garden City L.I. NY 11530

Appendix
Sources of Survival Equipment

Sporty's Pilot Shop
a division of Sportsmans Market
Clermont County Airport
Batavia, Ohio 45103

Eddie Bauer
P. O. Box 3700
Seattle, Washington 98124

L. L. Bean, Inc.
Freeport, Maine 04033

Chris Craft
Algonac, Michigan 48001

The Orvis Co. Inc.
Manchester, Vt. 05254

Norm Thompson
P.O. Box 3999
Portland , Oregon 97208

Charter Arms Corporation
430 Sniffens Lane
Stratford, Conneticut 06497

Savage Arms Division,
Emhart Industries, Inc.
Westfield, Massachussets 01085

Gokey's
84 South Wabasha St.
St. Paul, Minnesota 55107

For survival foods, both dehydrated and freeze-dried, consult your
nearest sporting goods dealer and the local supermarket.

And—don't forget Sears Roebuck!

Index

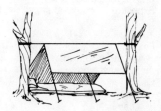

Index

A

Accidents	18
non-survivable	18
survivable	18
survivable aircraft	18
Airplane cabin as shelter	57
Airplane, staying in	57
Aluminum foil	53, 119
Aluminum foil, heavy duty	120
Ammunition	100
AOPA survival kit	43
Axe	75
cruising	76
hand	60
sheath	77

B

Barrel cactus	54
Berries	90
Birds	96
Briefing time	151
Bruises	38
Buck fever	113
Butchering	117

C

Call for help	156
Camp fire	41, 78
Camp fire, types	78
Canteen	53
Cargo nets	27
Caverns	60
Caves	60
Chain saw	76
Chill factor	67
Cleaning	115
large animals	116
procedures	115
small game	115
Climbing hills	138
Clothing	58
bed	73
cold weather	66
for survival	64
foul weather	58
goose down	68
hot weather	64-66
woolen	67
Colored smoke	88
Comfort at night	69
Compromises	49
Concussions	38
Cooking fire	78, 84
Cooking in the wilds	118
Cuts	38

D

Dead-falls	97
Deceleration, rapid & progressive	27

Dehydration	39
Deteriorating weather	21
Digestive system	51
Dilbert Dunker	147

E

ELT	41
Emergency landings	20
gentle	27
slow	27
types	22
Emergency locator	
transmitter	41
transmitter, does it work	169
Engine-roughness drill	24
Exposure problems at sea	158

F

Fear	16
of the unknown	34
unreasoning	16
Fire	34
basic need	74
camp	41, 78
cooking	78, 84
in the woods	75
-laying tools	75
-lighter	84
signalling	85
starting	79
starting, back-ups	81
Firearms	99
basic	99
basic hints	111
combination	104
morale factor	107
practice	114
First aid	35
course	36
kit	36
storage	36
First things first	41
Fish	
fresh	94
preparing	114
Fishing	94
rod	94
supplies	95
Flaps	28
Flares	176
Flare guns	176
Flashlight battery	83
Flight plans	166
Flint	82
Floatation	150
equipment	151
equipment, check	154

equipment, practice	155
gear	150
Food	34
assortment	124
availability	90
availability, local	90
from the sea	93
poisoning	38
required	89
Foot warmers	73
Forced landings	22
Frame	62

G

Gear	28
Gloves	68

H

Halazone tablets	52
Handguns	104
Head protection	158
Hershey bars	100
Housekeeping, basic instructions	40
Hunting	108
advice	108
bird	113
wildlife	111

I

Injuries	38
internal	38
spinal	38
typical	38
Illnesses, typical	38
Insect repellent	66
Iodine tablets	52

K

Kindling	75
Knife	78
sharpening	122
survival	121
Kodak film	100

L

Landings	20
emergency	20
forced	22
on treetops	28
pick your best spot	30
precautionary	22
survivable	26
unplanned	20
Life raft	152
Lighter, cricket-type	84
Log cabin fire	78
Luggage straps	27

M

Machette	60, 75
Magnetic compass	108, 142
Magnifying glass	82
Matches	79
kitchen	79
preparation	79
Mattresses	
air	73
foam rubber	70
Meat, fresh	96
Mechanical failures	20
Mental attitude	26
Mosquito netting	66

N

National Transportation Safety Board	18
Navigating on foot	140
Notes, always leave	142-146
NTSB	18

O

Outdoors, hazards	138
Outdoorsmen	134-136
Overdue alert	166
Overhangs, rocky	60

P

Panic	16
Parka, goose-down	68
Pay-off	168
Physiological problems	64
Pistols	105
cons	106
pros	105
Plumber's candle	84
Ponchos	58
Poopie suit	159
Portable	55
Pot-making improvisation	118
Precautionary landings	22
Psychological preparation	24

R

Radio communications, possible	172
Reality	16
Reconstitutable food	56, 124-126
Rifles	99-102
Rockets	176
Roots	90
Rubberized rain suits	58

S

Sea food	91
Sea food, cooking	92
Seasickness	162
Security devices	27
Seeds	90
Shears	60
Shellfish	91
Shelter	33
lean-to construction	58
natural	60
Shock	38
Shock treatment	38
Shotgun	102-103
Signalling	41
devices	41, 163
fire	85
Skinning	117
Sleeping bags	70
air out	72
bedshaped	72
goose-down	72
rectangular	72
types	72
Small game	96
preparing	114
Smoke, colored	88
Snares	97
Snow	52
Solar stills	53
Socks	68
Splash down	157
after	157
just wait	162
Sprains	38
Star fire	78
Steel	82
Steel wool	83
Stoves	84
Sterno	84
types	85
Sublimation	68
Sunburn	64
Survivable	18
aircraft accidents	18
landing	26
landings, conclusions	32
Survival	
kit, aircraft	128
kit, AOPA	43
author's grab bag	46-48, 128-133
kit, basic	42
commercial basic	42
Delta bag	48
fair weather	128
kit for heavy going	48
kit, Piper bag	46
kit, sizes	42
requirements	33
Survivor IV	48

T

Tarp	64, 86
Teepee fire	78

Telephone calls, personal	167
Tents	61
backpackers	62
basic protection	61
cabin type	62
grommets	63
materials made out of	62
mountain climbers	62
pup	62
short-term emergency	64
tube	62
Terra firma	22
Tinder	75
Tinder, keep dry	82
Thinking ahead	16
Tools	
edged	77
fire-laying	75
Traps	97
Turtles	92
Turtles, cooking	92

U

Underwear, fishnet	67
Unplanned landings	20

V

Visual signals, close-in	173

W

Water	33
availability	52
boiling before drinking	52
conservation	52
daily requirement	51
holes	55
Water imbalance	39
in the desert	53
markers	165
purify	52
sources, desert	54
the need for	51
Walking	137
mechanics	137
the rough	137
Whistle	110
Wilderness, what is	17
Wood, wet	82
Wooded areas	60
Wool	67